Just a
Moment

Just a Moment

Life Matters
with Father Tom

MONSIGNOR THOMAS HARTMAN

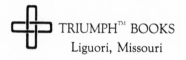

TRIUMPH™ BOOKS
Liguori, Missouri

Published by Triumph™ Books
Liguori, Missouri
An Imprint of Liguori Publications

Most scriptural citations are from *The New American Bible*,
copyright © 1970 by the Confraternity of Christian Doctrine,
Washington, D.C. Revised New Testament, © 1986.

Library of Congress Cataloging-in-Publication Data

Hartman, Thomas.
   Just a moment—life matters with Father Tom /
   Thomas Hartman. — 1st ed.
   222 p.   cm.
   ISBN 0-89243-530-5 : $12.95
   1. Meditations. 2. Hartman, Thomas. I. Title.
BX2182.2.H37   1993
242—dc20   92-43420
                                     CIP

Printed in the United States of America.

First Edition

Contents

A Note of Thanks to Joe Cook

In many respects, this book was Joe's idea. He's an expert on the short-form essay for television and radio, and was my guiding light. Joe's credentials are amazing. He wrote and produced over five hundred broadcast essays for the late Harry Reasoner during their days at ABC, and he's written scores of major TV shows for ABC, NBC and CBS. He scripted hundreds of episodes of the children's series, "The Great Space Coaster," and won the prestigious Peabody Award for this work. He took Walt Disney's *Snow White* from the screen and put it on the stages of the Radio City Music Hall and the St. Louis Municipal Opera. His shows have played the biggest halls, including Carnegie, and he still found time to script the Miss America Pageant on NBC for eight consecutive years. He's the most prolific television showman I've ever known. Space limits his long list of credits, but I must add that his wife, Rosemary, a Minister of Music and for many years organist and head of the choir at Our Lady of Victory Church in Floral Park, New York, suggested the title of this book. So let me take *Just a Moment* to say thank you.

Foreword

Just a Moment was born during a rather rapid ride from the Telicare cable studios in Uniondale, Long Island, to New York City where I was scheduled to attend a script session on a television project of some magnitude. I asked a friend of mine to come along. He had written and produced hundreds of such shows and I felt his input would be valuable. As we drove toward the city I mentioned that I had to make a stop in Great Neck, a village on the north shore. He didn't mind; he was just going along for the ride, he said.

As I pulled into the rectory parking lot at St. Aloysius parish, he asked, "You're going to light a candle for the script session?"

"No, I'm going to say a funeral mass for a good friend," I told him. I invited him to wait for me in the sacristy.

When the mass ended and we had returned to the car to continue our trip to New York, he sat silently for a few moments and then said, "You give a great funeral. I don't know who the lady was, but I could see the reaction of her family and that's the way I'd want to leave if I were Catholic."

"Being a Catholic really has nothing to do with it," I said. Then I told him about this young woman, who'd left behind a husband and three beautiful children.

What he couldn't quite get over, it seemed, was the fact that while I was in charge of a rather extensive television operation for my diocese, I still fulfilled my "priestly duties."

"You still have time for funerals, weddings, baptisms...?"

"And hospital calls, prison visits, marriage consultations, Sunday sermons..."

"Where do you find time?" he asked.

"I make the time. This is what I do. I'm a working priest."

"I don't think I could handle it," he said. "The Writer's Guild wouldn't stand for the hours. Or the money."

Writers are, of necessity, very curious people. He asked me how I handled the problems of families in crisis—battered women, alcoholism, kids in trouble. Then he asked me the big one: "What do priests think about?"

"When you pick up the morning paper," he asked, "what goes through your mind? When you turn on the TV news in the morning, what are you thinking? How real is your God? How closely do you look at everyday things? What joy do you get out of spending your whole life just trying to help other people? How can you stay in the priesthood with so many terrific attractions all around you?"

Of course, there was no pat answer as to how I viewed the world. I would have to take my reactions item by item, event by event.

Then he said, as writers do, "You ought to keep a sort of diary. Put some of your thoughts down."

As our long association continued, we spent many pleasant hours regaling each other with events in our lives over coffee or during a ride to a television location, or while working on scripts.

And each time I told him about something that moved me to any degree at all, he would say, "Write it down. Keep it fresh and share it." So I started making notes—which often turned into stories. As time went by, he suggested putting my thoughts on the air in what he called "little moments." And, indeed, some of the thoughts in this volume actually did end up on television.

I believe we can learn a lot from stories. Like everyone else, a priest reacts to everything that goes on around him, to the conversations he has, the stories he reads, and the stories he hears. In this collage of special "moments" that have impressed me there is a mixture of short-short homilies, slices of true life, and reflections of personal happenings.

For the most part, these are everyday stories of love and faith, each one carrying, in its own way, the attitude of hope. In most respects, these stories are quiet testimonies that God has a plan or purpose. Some of these stories concern difficult moments in people's lives. And truly difficult moments do happen to all of us.

But mostly they are simple observations of a working priest who has been inspired by a friend. I hope you enjoy them.

"When I was young, I said to God, 'God, tell me the mystery of the universe.' But God answered, 'That knowledge is reserved for me alone.' So I said, 'God, tell me the mystery of the peanut.' Then God said, 'Well, George, that's more nearly your size.' And he told me."

—George Washington Carver

The Bird and the Crocodile

*P*icture this. A terrifyingly huge crocodile emerges from the muddy waters of a swamp. He opens his viselike jaws wide, displaying rows of teeth that would absolutely destroy any living thing. A little red bird flies to the huge reptile—a bird the size of a robin. It lands on the crocodile's lower jaw, inside its mouth.

The huge mouth remains open—and it will not close while the little bird is there because the bird is actually performing periodontal work on the crocodile's gums, removing the leeches that meant pain for the crocodile but a great meal for the bird.

A little moth that never saw its mother hunts for a flower it has never seen. Its body is the exact length necessary to lay its eggs in the bloom—not far enough to interfere with the seed, but far enough to be enclosed in the outer shell. When the baby wakes up with a ravenous appetite, it finds a perfect balanced diet in a succulent layer between the seed and the shell.

Now, what person planned all this? The arrangement between the crocodile and the little red bird? Who arranged for the baby moth to find the flower? Who decided that green plants should breathe in carbon dioxide and emit oxygen to make our earth livable?

No person. These are the wonders of our creator, and we can only try to duplicate what God has put all around us. We can fly only because God's birds taught us how. Whether in a microcosm of life or in the grandeur of a great ocean, we see His work.

Psalm 19:1 says it this way: "The heavens declare the glory of God, and the firmament proclaims his handiwork."

Love on the
Refrigerator Door

I was reading a press release the other day about the transmission of thoughts of love and affection by means of greetings cards and was somewhat amazed to find out what a big business cards have become.

The first valentines appeared in America in 1849 —and Christmas cards have been around since shortly after the printing press was invented.

According to the Hallmark people, who sell more cards than anybody, Americans buy more than 900 million valentines a year—card sales second only to Christmas. But the fancy little five-or-ten-cent cards of yesterday now start at about $1.25. A really nice birthday card can run you about $3.50. Yes, printed love is getting pretty expensive —especially when you add another 29 cents (at least) for a stamp.

There's another way to say "I love you." A little girl gave her mother the most wonderful greeting card in the world—and she didn't spend a nickel for it. Someplace she found some paper. It was nice paper that somebody was going to throw out. Then she got out the stubs of some crayons she had in a little tin box—three colors: red, green, and purple. And she drew a stick figure with a round head in the middle of the paper. And because it was her mother, she gave it a fine hairdo. Then came the big block letters. Four words. *Mother. I love you.* And she signed it in real handwriting.

This was the card that made it to the site of honor . . .the refrigerator door. This is the card her mother will see and love a hundred times a day.

The Gift of Time

*H*er parents had given her the best education money could buy. She excelled in her field and became a tremendous success in business.

She knew her parents had worked hard to get together the wherewithall to allow her to concentrate only on her schooling and career. She never had to work during her college days. As her bank account grew, she made sure her parents had the best of everything. The best television set, the best VCR, the best silverware. And last winter, a car.

Sounds very nice, doesn't it? But her parents really could have done *without* the best of everything if only she would have given them something they really wanted—a few minutes of her time. A visit where they just sat and talked. It would have been nice, they thought, if instead of just giving them good seats for the theater, she *took* them there. If, instead of telegraphing a huge floral arrangement for their anniversary, she brought it to them—and a smaller arrangement would have done nicely. It would have been even better.

A mother I once counseled said, "Things are nice. It's very convenient to have 'things'—but it's nicer to have children and friends who care enough to spend a little of their valuable time with you." How right she was.

I recall visiting an elderly parishioner in a nursing home. He awoke very early, got all dressed up, and had managed to get one of the care-providers to sneak out and buy him two little boxes of candy. These were to be for the grandchildren when they came with his daughter and son-in-law to visit. The first time in over a month. His face glowed.

Then he was called to the phone. He looked solemn when he returned to his room. It seems there was this soccer game, and his daughter had forgotten about the ballet lesson, but maybe they could make it next week.

Time, my friends. It costs so little and means so much.

Giving Love Away

*O*scar Hammerstein II wrote a lyric for which there was no melody, and one night he sent this hand-written poem to Mary Martin just before she went onstage in a performance of *South Pacific*.

Oscar Hammerstein was on his deathbed at the time, but he wanted Mary to know how he felt about her—both professionally and personally.

The note said:

Dear Mary,
A bell's not a bell until you ring it.
A song's not a song until you sing it.
Love in your heart is not put there to stay.
Love isn't love until you give it away.

Mary Martin said she gave the performance of her life that night. And when someone asked her about the energy, the skill, and the magnificence of that performance, she showed the note and said, "Tonight I gave my love away."

Today, love is often confused with other things—friendliness, charity, physical desire. In the Bible, Peter speaks differently about love. He says, "Love one another intensely from a [pure] heart." (1 Peter 1:22). He asks that we avoid being hypocritical when we talk about love. Some people feign love. They put on a mask, much the way an actor hides behind a character. That person's love is not love at all.

Consider the circumstances of the Mary Martin note. A man is dying. Whatever this performer had to do with his success is now a moot point. He can take nothing with him. He can ask nothing of this woman. As successful and rich as he had become, the only thing he could offer now is his appreciation and his love. He gave it to her and she gave it to the world.

A Little Note of Kindness

*H*ow long does it take to write a one-line note? Not long. Have we any idea how just a few words can lift someone's spirit or warm someone's heart? How many times have you said, "I should drop a note to Frank or to Eileen and tell them how good they are." And you don't.

It's an unusual phenomenon. For the most part, people seem to be in a demolition derby. Maybe it's because there's so much criticism around. For some reason it's so much easier to tear something down than to build it up. . .just as it seems so much easier to frown than it is to smile.

Listen to any conversation carefully. I mean *any* conversation. If you go by the people who are speaking, nothing in the world is right and nobody is much good at anything.

Well, I'll admit that life can be sad and life can be full of frustrations, and there will always be good guys and bad guys—in varying degrees of goodness and badness. But there is a dearth of what I call Appreciators—people who see or hear something good and simply appreciate it—to the extent that they will actually take a pen and jot down a few words of praise to someone else.

Did you ever get a little note of that kind? Remember how it absolutely made your day? How good you felt? It might have been one sentence. Or a few words like, "You're great!" Making others feel good about themselves will make us feel good, too.

Forget the fancy stationery or the literary content—
just remember to remember.

In Proverbs 15:13 we read: "A glad heart lights
up the face." And joy is a two-way street.

Choices

*A*ll of our lives we make choices. We can choose the paths our lives will take. We can choose our mates. We can choose just about anything we want to choose, as long as it's not illegal, immoral, or fattening. And, even there, it's of our own choosing.

But the most important choices of our lives are really the easiest choices—why they seem so difficult is hard to understand. Follow me with this reasoning: Is it easier to choose to *love* rather than *hate*? Take your choice—is it easier to *smile* than to *growl*? Why do so many people find it a lot easier to destroy than to build?

- You can choose to persevere rather than quit.
- You can choose to praise rather than gossip.
- You can choose to heal rather than hurt.
- You can choose to give, rather than take away.
- You can choose to act rather than delay.
- You can choose to forgive rather than carry a grudge.
- You can choose to pray rather than despair.

Those are the really *big* choices. Those choices should be almost automatic. It depends on how you build them into your way of thinking.

There are two ways to look at that list of choices. First, any one of them will make you feel good... feel *really* good about yourself. Then, too, I can't think of a truly successful individual who hasn't made those choices along the way. Take just one word out of each suggestion and you have the makings of one of God's most powerful personalities: Love...smile   ...build...persevere...praise... heal...give... act...forgive...and pray.

You can choose to do any or all of these things, and it won't cost you a dime.

Solitude

*P*rofessional songwriters know that, when all else fails, write a "lonesome" song...like Elvis Presley's "Are You Lonesome Tonight?" A lot of people like the "lonesome" idea. It helps them become sad. Believe it or not some people are really into sadness.

But they could turn loneliness into something positive called "solitude." Solitude is what psychiatrists call "the proper use of being alone." This is the real enjoyment of being away from others. Otto Wolfgang, a psychologist, says there can be pleasure, excitement, and exhilaration in solitude.

We spend our lives making adjustments—in school, at work, on committees, even at church—and certainly in any male-female relationship. But in our solitude we can recapture our real selves, without conformity, without social discipline, without affectation. We can even pray out loud!

The trouble is that some people worry so much about why they're alone that they get very anxious. Solitude is the time to think. Too often we let the television set, newspapers, and books do our thinking for us. Solitude, when it's used correctly, can awaken you to the beautiful details of life. The smell of a summer morning...the ticking of the clock... the sounds of life. Solitude can be a terrific change of pace. All your working life, you'll be busy making money, raising a family, saving for retirement—and you might not realize that it takes a little solitude to recharge the batteries.

So, when you're alone, don't panic and think, *What's wrong with me?* Say, "Hey, this is great. I've got some time for myself!"

You'll be surprised how—suddenly—the problems that have been bothering you all day will become clearer.

One Day at a Time

*P*oliticians, philosophers, and advertising agency executives talk frequently about "the big picture." But when most of us try to contemplate our entire lives or to think about all our problems at once, the process becomes overwhelming. The tasks seem monumental, the problems too complex to solve.

So, take it one day at a time. And if that seems too much, take things an hour at a time. Here's a little philosophy that may help. Say to yourself:

I will take this one day at a time. I can do something for twelve hours that would appall me if I had to keep it up for a lifetime.

Just for today I will adjust myself to what *is*, and forget my own desires.

Just for today I will exercise my soul in three ways. I will do somebody good; I will do two things that I don't want to do; and I will forgive someone who may have hurt me.

Just for today I will be unafraid. I will believe that as I give to the world, God will give to me.

Just for today I will avoid a bad habit. I will realize why I must.

Just for today I will save myself from hurry and indecision.

Just for today I will realize that not everything will turn out just the way I want it to, but I won't let it bother me.

Just for today I will look at the other side of any situation that annoys me and try to understand it.

If you can live with that philosophy for just one day, you're on your way to a remarkable week—and month and year. As the Book of Matthew (6:34) says: "Let the day's own trouble be sufficient for the day."

Einstein and God

I was driving through Princeton on my way home to Long Island the other day, and the spectre of Albert Einstein seemed to loom over the campus. He was, after all, their most prestigious faculty member at one time.

Einstein was best known, of course, for his theory of relativity. And he seemed to think it was perfectly understandable to anyone. $E=MC^2$—Energy equals mass times the volocity of light, squared.

Einstein was the one who put "time" into the mix, which was a new idea at the time, and he explained it this way: "When you're courting a nice girl, an hour seems like a second. When you sit on a hot radiator, a second seems like an hour."

I wondered how one of the world's greatest scientists and mathematicians felt about God. Here was a mind that could figure out things about our universe that others couldn't *begin* to fathom. In all his explorations, did Einstein find God?

Well, let's examine his philosophy. Dr. Einstein said: "The most beautiful thing we can experience is the mysterious. It is the source of all true art and science." He also said: "Imagination is more important than knowledge," and "God is subtle—but he is not malicious. We should take great care not to make the *intellect* our god." Intellect, he concluded, "has powerful muscles . . . but no personality. Only God is God."

One of Einstein's most-quoted statements gets truer by the year: "The hardest thing in the world to understand is—the income tax." But God he could perceive.

Criticism

You join a community project—a club or a service organization. After a few weeks, you're talked into becoming a member of a committee. At first you demur, then you accept. You feel you should really be more active than you have been. You enjoy committee work; you are complimented on your dedication.

But pretty soon there are murmers of discontent from other members. You sense they're talking about you behind your back. Then you hear some direct criticism about your handling of things. You really tried, so the criticism hurts. Your first inclination is to throw up your hands and quit. Who needs it?

Well, if it's not constructive criticism, nobody needs it. Yet in every group, large or small, in every situation, at work or in the community—or even at home—you'll find a critic. People like to harp. Especially those people who see other people get a little credit for something.

I was talking with a very disillusioned television personality one day and he was saying, "I don't know why it is, but when you first come on the scene, everybody adores you. You can do no wrong. But when you become well-known—when you get good publicity, when people stop you on the street, this is the time when they want to tear you down. It seems like a game that all people play."

The game is centuries old. No one was ever more adored or more maligned than our Lord. His was the classic case. Just remember: If you're not being criticized, you're not doing anything.

If you need a word to comfort you, try this—from Matthew 5:44: "Love your enemies, and pray for those who persecute you."

And I say, don't quit. Keep doing good things. Even the rose has thorns...and criticism goes with the territory.

Little Things Mean a Lot

*T*ouch my hand when you pass my chair," was a line in a great pop tune of the fifties that represented the deepest wishes of many a family member. The song was called "Little Things Mean a Lot"—and in truth, they still do.

Sometimes we forget, completely forget, the most important people in our lives—our wives, our husbands, our sons and daughters, our mothers and fathers. Let me ask a rather obtuse question: Can you think of anything you *like* about your parents? Your children? Your fellow workers? Certainly. But when was the last time you *said* so? You don't have to make up things. You don't have to lie. You just have to look—and see. That's the trick. Actually seeing.

In the Thornton Wilder play *Our Town*, there's a very touching scene in which Emily comes back after death to relive her fourteenth birthday, and she sees her father and mother and how they looked and acted on that beautiful day. And Emily cries out, "Mother, you're so young! Daddy, look at Mother. Please look and see how young and wonderful she is. She'll be gone soon. Please—look at each other."

We pass our family and friends so many times a day that we just don't see them. But they are there—and deep inside them there is truly a crying need to be noticed, to be talked to, to be touched, to be loved.

In this age of awesome technology, we can communicate in ways never before imagined. But do we communicate where the need is really the greatest? Do we still remember our beloved in our prayers? We must, because this reflects the grace and glory of a loving God.

"Listen My Children..."

*H*enry Wadsworth Longfellow laid it right on the line when he started his epic poem "Paul Revere's Ride" with the words, "Listen my children and you shall hear..." The key word there is *listen*. In the American rat race, there is a growing habit of hearing but not listening. We're always on the go, and we don't seem to have the *time* to listen.

In a survey that asked a thousand young women what they looked for in an ideal man, very high on the list was, "Someone who listens." Some non-listeners have an answer for that. The person who's talking is boring. "She rambles on and I turn her off," or, "He never *says* anything."

That says you're probably not a very good listener, because a good listener knows that you can sense feelings, body language, and eye contact that will tell you as much as words do.

There are a few simple rules for becoming a world-class listener. Don't finish someone's sentence even if you know what he's going to say. It smacks of impatience. Let the speaker finish...Don't jump in with a thought of your own before someone can finish hers. Or his. Show interest. It's the most flattering thing you can do. People who show interest very often find something that really *is* interesting ...Don't be an habitual topper. A conversation isn't a battle of who's the best. It's simply an exchange of pleasantries and information...Ask questions if you don't understand. It shows you actually are interested—and are listening.

In the Book of Job (21: 1,2) we read: "At least listen to my words...bear with me while I speak."

One thing is certain: Being a good listener will make you everyone's best friend.

Winning and Losing

*A*mericans have an obsession with winning. We want to find out who's in the top ten of anything. It's important to know who won the Oscars...who won the Grammys...what team won the pennant. The lists are endless, but the concern is always: who won?

The late Vince Lombardi said, "Winning isn't everything. It's the *only* thing." Leo Durocher said, "Nice guys finish last." So, how does this affect us?

Penelope Leach, writing in the *New York Times* about parents who desperately want their children to win, said, "Childhood today is too hurried and fast. Development is a process, not a race. To me," she says, "the most important thing one can give a child is genuine, unconditional love. That is what self-esteem and self-confidence are founded on. When you push a child to do things early or to be the best at gymnastics or dancing class, you imply: 'I love you more when you win.' That," she says, is very damaging."

I've met with a lot of people who suffer from extreme anxiety because they worry about how they're perceived by others. They worry about what people will think of them if they don't achieve success —if they don't "win." How awful it would be if they failed. It's not only a real worry, it's a worry that can upset your life, and in some cases actually destroy it. Any truly successful athlete can tell you that you cannot allow other people to determine

your behavior. Fears and pressures that most people experience are usually external. You don't have
to win every time.

Remember, God rewards honest effort—and your
reward will be peace of mind.

Thomas Jefferson's
"Nevers"

I'm sure we all agree that the Declaration of Independence is a masterful piece of writing. It was the work of a young man who would become our third president, Thomas Jefferson. But that's not all he wrote. He also gave his granddaughter, on her twelfth birthday, a list of what he called The Canons of Conduct in Life:

- Never put off to tomorrow what you can do today.
- Never trouble another if you can do it yourself.
- Never spend your money before you have it.
- Never buy a thing you do not want because it's cheap.
- Take care of your cents. The dollars will take care of themselves.
- Pride costs more than hunger, thirst, and cold.
- Never repent of eating too little.
- Nothing is troublesome that one does willingly.
- Take things always by their smooth handle.
- When angry, count to ten before you speak. If very angry, count to one hundred.

In the early days, such maxims were very popular. They were taught in schools, along with "readin', ritin', and 'rithmetic." They show high regard for the virtues of perseverance, moderation, patience, dietary habits, and respect for others. Jefferson's "Nevers" number only ten. They aren't commandments, but wouldn't the world be a great place if we thought of them that way?

I am often awed by the principles of our founding fathers. Their rationale, their foresight, their ability to put down on paper ideologies that would change the world for centuries to come—and all in the name of the Lord.

One Small Voice

*E*very Christmas we hear the story of the Little Drummer Boy who says in song, "Baby Jesus, I am a poor boy, too. I have no gift to bring that's fit to give our king. Shall I play for you on my drum?"

The wonderful story these lines tell is that there is no gift or gesture too small if it pleases the Lord. We often wonder, what can one person do? What difference will my little contribution make? Mother Teresa of Calcutta, a woman who has challenged the conscience of the entire world, said, "What we are doing is just a drop in the ocean, but if that drop was not in the ocean, I think the ocean would be missing that drop."

I have never known of any true humanitarian or philosopher who hasn't echoed that sentiment. One of the most serious thoughts that life provokes is this: We can never tell when a word, a look, an occurrence of any kind is trivial or important.

There are so many bromides on the subject. "In the joy of little things, the heart finds the morning and is refreshed." Or simply consider the often-quoted Bible story of the mustard seed that someone planted in the field. It's the smallest seed that someone planted in the field. It's the smallest of all seeds, but when grown, it's the greatest of shrubs and becomes a tree.

Very often we are aching to help someone, but are afraid what little help we could give would mean nothing. Take the problem of poverty, for instance.

It is so immense in this world that we are awestruck by it. Yet we mustn't think whatever contribution we can make would be too small.

Be it a penny or a prayer, reach out. You can make a difference.

Dealing with Difficult People

*W*e all know at least one—co-worker, neighbor, employee, or boss who really gets our stomach churning. Dealing with difficult people is...difficult. If you think you're going to explode, you might try one of these strategies, courtesy of the Scripps-Howard News Service.

First, don't take the conflict personally. Watch that difficult person with others, and you'll see that he or she is just as impossible with nearly everyone.

Also, consider the personality type you're dealing with. There's the Attacker, the Know-it-all, the Back Stabber, the Complainer, the Clam, or the garden variety Snake in the Grass. Take a little time to figure out *how* that person operates so you can predict his or her behavior and plan a response. However, don't devote all your waking hours to this, because you'll end up at your doctor's office.

Most important, take special notice of why that person is bothering you. Then, they suggest, force the person to get to the heart of the issue. Make him or her explain outrageous statements. Make him stick to the facts—you don't want to deal with emotions, only the facts. And—this is very important—*rehearse* your meeting. Talk it out to yourself in the car on the way to work, for instance. See if you can't clear the air.

Above all, don't write off somebody as being impossible because of a few unpleasant episodes. Instead, try the Lord's suggestion: Pray for the person. And if you really want to put a cap on outbursts, *tell* him you'll pray for him. Then do it.

The late Bishop Fulton Sheen said it this way, "If true peace is to be won, it must first be won in our own hearts." Difficult people can give us a good chance to test the power of prayer.

Ultimatums

On my way to work one morning, I saw two grown men having a furious fight over a parking space. They were throwing ultimatums back and forth as though it were the beginning of World War III. I have no idea who won the parking space, because I didn't stop and turn it into a spectator sport. But it did start me thinking.

We Americans use ultimatums more than any group of citizens I've ever encountered anywhere. We have developed a sort of dictatorial attitude in situations where we feel we are being bruised, cheated, scorned or rejected. We seem to be totally unable to accept being the least bit inconvenienced. We want to be in charge.

There are some basic rules about ultimatums. You should use them very sparingly. The other person must know that what you say is very important to you...You should resort to an ultimatum only when nothing else works...And when you decide to issue one, act calm and cool, not desperate... Don't let yourself get trapped in an argument, because if you do, your ultimatum goes out the window...And when you issue your ultimatum, be prepared to deal with the *worst response*.

For example, if a young woman tells her boyfriend that if he doesn't marry her before Christmas she'll never see him again... chances are pretty good that she'll never see him again.

Take a tip from our Lord, "Whoever exalts himself, will be humbled; but whoever humbles himself will be exalted." (Matthew 23:12)

If you're looking for an example of a great ultimatum, here's one from the Book of Luke 14:27. "Whoever does not carry his own cross and come after me cannot be my disciple."

Having Patience

If patience is a virtue, or, if it's true that patience is its own reward, then we all had better take some patience lessons. Schools should teach a short course in patience. In this hurry-scurry world, with so much to do and so many places to be, the technical side of our civilization has some built-in "patience-tryers"

A firm called Priority Management, Incorporated, has done a time and motion study that tells us that in a lifetime, the average American will spend six months waiting at stoplights. Six months. That same individual will spend eight months opening junk mail. We'll spend a whole year just looking for things we've misplaced. The average American will spend two whole years unsuccessfully returning phone calls and four years doing housework. But the topper is this: In our lifetime, we will spend five years waiting in line!

The interesting part about waiting in traffic, standing in line, or looking for lost objects is that we consider this to be downtime...wasted time, time in which we could be doing something "constructive." What's amazing about it is that we have figured out how to fill practically every second of our days and nights, but haven't come up with a solution to our downtime.

No time to think? To sort out the things that trouble you? Do it when you're in a line at the bank. No time for French lessons? Pop in a cassette while you're waiting for the light to change. No time for a prayer for a loved one? I think God would okay a few prayers while we're doing housework. The exasperation, the numbing nervousness will disappear when you have something more to think about than how fast the line is moving.

Let me offer a paraphrased thought to help you: "Do not covet thy neighbor's place in line." It will do you no good. Think other thoughts and you will overcome.

The Ten Suggestions

I wonder how many adults can still recite the Ten Commandments. It used to be a standard exercise in almost every church school.

These days, many people—even the most influential—and many of the most famous, have chipped away at the Ten Commandments and regard them more or less as "The Ten Suggestions." That won't really do.

I came across a new set of commandments that could easily be amended to the original ten to give these orders a hip, modern flavor:

- Honor your Lord all the days of your life, and your children will grow up and bless you.
- Remember to say "I Love You." For though your love may be constant, your family yearns to hear these words.
- Keep your home in good repair, for out of it comes the joy of old age.
- Take time for prayer, it will sustain you in the difficult times.
- Do not abuse your body with excessive food or drink, so that you may live long and be healthy in the presence of those you love.
- Put your mate before your mother, your father, your son, and your daughter, for your mate is your lifelong companion.

- Remember always that the approval of your mate is worth more than the admiring glances of a hundred strangers...so remain faithful.
- Dedicate yourself to good causes and helping others.
- Appreciate nature while working to preserve the environment.
- Forgive with grace...for who among us doesn't need to be forgiven?

Well, they're not commandments, but they're mighty good suggestions.

Love and Business

*N*ever in the history of journalism has the business section of the daily paper been read by so many people. Business sections hold as much fascination as the comics used to. Here is where the game of greed is played. Here we find the harbingers of mass layoffs, leveraged buyouts, charts that tell us we're in deep trouble.

Manufacturing plants closing down after reporting billions of dollars in losses. Companies on the edge issuing a hiring freeze. The teenage job market falling apart. Big banks with big problems.

Now, I don't claim to be a financial expert, but I do hear many comments on what seems to be causing all this attention to business matters. Bad ideas and bad debts. Which, of course, are caused by a tremendous rush to become as rich as possible as quickly as possible.

Of course, we've all heard the old adage, power corrupts—and absolute power corrupts absolutely. How does all this square with the idea of morality and conscience? It doesn't. If greed causes harm to one's fellowman, it's as immoral as physical injury ...perhaps moreso.

Explain to a laid-off factory worker why the chairman of the company that fired him has to have a $7 million salary because he can't get along on five. Maybe we should recall the advice in Matthew 6:19: "Do not store up for yourselves treasures on earth." That's a line you won't find quoted much on the business pages. As while we believe that the rich man's riches will someday turn to dust—as will the man himself—we have to live with his compulsion to amass money.

So we must find our riches around ourselves. Look about and recognize those who love you and care for you . . . because these are your riches. There isn't enough money in the world to buy love. The power broker should be so lucky.

Words, Words, Words...

*I*n two minutes on television a commentator will use about two hundred fifty words. A twenty-eight minute newscast contains about three thousand words.

Imagine how many words a day fly through the air from the thousands of radio and television stations in this country alone. Billions of words every day. Billions more appear in print in the newspapers, magazines, and books.

It seems these words from all the media are more often trying to sell you something or entertain you than inform you. Sometimes these words are created to confuse or even deceive you. It seems we could easily drown in this daily flood of words. And if there are a billion words today, there will be another billion words tomorrow.

Just think a moment. It's been less than a hundred years since we've been able to produce so many words. The typewriter wasn't considered practical until 1893. There was no radio then, let alone television. Books were scarce, and magazines were read only by people who could read, and they weren't in the majority. Now, with the proliferation of words, we have thousands upon thousands of writers for radio and TV who are writing words that are written to be forgotten.

One word has transcended the centuries. It was the basic book for scholars. The Bible. The Word of God. Words written to be remembered—no noisy fanfare, no headline teases, and no commercials.

In Isaiah 55:10, 11 we read: "Just as from the heavens the rain and snow come down and do not return there till they have watered the earth, making it fruitful...so shall my word be that goes forth from my mouth. It shall not return to me void, but shall do my will, achieving the end for which I sent it."

So said the Lord in a few well-chosen words that will live forever.

Politics Is Usual

*N*o matter where you look—whether it be in a factory, an office, a school, a great university, or, yes, even a parish—you'll find the ugly "p" word. *Politics.* Characterized, Webster says, "by shrewdness in managing, contriving, or dealing—or being sagacious in promoting a policy."

Politics in the workplace is based on the notion that somebody's getting something you're not getting and if you could bring that person down, surely you would win the day and be happier and richer. That might be an oversimplification, but it's pretty much what politics is all about.

The problem with politics is not so much that it becomes an office game, but that it is a game that hurts and sometimes destroys good people. It's part of a system that dictates that everybody has a boss. Even the boss has a boss. And the idea of the game is to find yourself in good favor with someone who can give you greater esteem and power and, if possible, a better life-style.

The late drama critic George Jean Nathan said, "Politics is the diversion of trivial people who, when they succeed at it, become important in the eyes of more trivial people."

The trouble with politics is that it is played with a lethal amount of venom. The idea is to kill off the competition, or knock off someone in authority. It starts with small, cutting remarks, small slights, and it grows into libelous accusations, allegations without proof, if any proof can even be expected.

Worst of all it is judgment by people who are unworthy to judge. In Matthew 7:1, 2 we read, "Stop judging, that you may be be judged. For as you judge, so will you be judged, and the measure with which you measure will be measured out to you."

So let the eternal boss do the judging. This isn't politics; it's gospel.

Time Out!

*I*t's nice to be busy. It's nice to be able to make things happen. But there are many people who are "busy by compulsion." If they're not doing something—if they're not operating at fever pitch—if they're just sitting down, they feel guilty.

Such people seem to have one big problem: They don't know how to rest. Instead, they push to achieve at work, at hobbies, and at sports. They fill their calendars with "activities." Gotta do this. Gotta do that. Gotta be here. Gotta be there.

Psychologists tell us that this adds to the stress syndrome and doesn't do us any good at all. When you suddenly discover that you have some free time, make yourself do nothing. Sit under a tree. Lie on the sofa. Find a comfortable chair and resist—*resist*—the urge to work or achieve anything. Or go to a quiet public place like the neighborhood church, or a beach, or a park—and leave your watch at home. Lean back. Look at the people. Remind yourself you're not trying to achieve anything. Or go for a drive or a walk without any set destination. Stop at interesting places.

If you're stuck in traffic, look up at the clouds. Look around at the scenery. Find a good radio program. Keep in mind that the time you spend not doing anything is actually very productive. You're recharging your batteries.

Just as you need sleep at night, you need breaks during the day. . .what I call "nothing breaks." And don't feel guilty. Instead of thinking about the things that need to be done, concentrate on the things you've *accomplished* and tell yourself, "I need this break."

And you might thank the good Lord for giving you the strength to rest.

Improving Your Image

---

*A*ccording to psychologists, many people are doing things that absolutely wreck their images—and they don't even know they're doing them.

Dr. Lillian Glass, a California psychologist, has made a list of the ten worst habits you can have . . . all of which can be corrected. She says you can improve your image in the eyes of your bosses, fellow workers, and friends if you take a good look at yourself. The ten worst habits are

1. Swearing or cursing. Most people don't say much about it, but it really turns a lot of people off. You come across as vulgar.
2. Acting childish. Women should stop the baby-girl voice, and men should put a lid on the temper tantrums.
3. Poor posture. Hunching over makes you look weak and insecure.
4. Talking too much. You come across as self-centered and boring.
5. Speaking in a monotone. Spice up your voice and become more interesting.
6. Being a poor listener. Pay attention to what the other person is really saying.
7. Frowning a lot. You come across as mean, grouchy, and critical. It may merely be self-consciousness on your part, but it gives a bad impression.
8. Speaking too loudly. You sound boisterous.

9. Just the opposite—speaking too softly.
10. Poor eye contact. It doesn't seem like much but it's important.

In the Bible is the admonition that we do unto others as we would have them do unto us. I would add "*Be* unto others." And, "*See* thyself."

How to Be Happy

*There's a song that goes, "I want to be happy." It speaks for everybody. Hundreds of volumes have come off the presses telling us how to be happy. They all say pretty much the same things. I've boiled down a few of these tomes, and here is the essence.

First, understand your own values and make sure they're your own and not somebody else's. Don't be swayed by advertising or what your friends say.

Second, accept people as they *are*; don't label them or classify them. Be tolerant of them.

Third, show a real interest in the lives of others. You'll learn something. And, also, caring adds to the enrichment of your own life. Be flexible and try to learn from your own experiences.

Fourth, be true to yourself and be willing to pay the consequences for living by your own values. That's what Christ did, you know.

Fifth, don't worry about what other people will think of you. It will slow you down and frustrate you, and you'll lead a very fearful life.

Sixth, don't be afraid to be emotionally moved by life. Try to appreciate the beauty of nature and, especially, children. People who can't be moved by emotions generally have already decided that people can't be trusted—or that people are no good. How many unhappy people do you know who act like that?

Seventh, express your own unique personality. It isn't necessary—or even wise—to conform all the time so that you will be just like everybody else. How do you know that everybody else is right?

An emotionally healthy person certainly respects the limitations of society and its rules. But an emotionally healthy person also doesn't look for or demand an answer to everything, but believes that God is our refuge and our strength.

Sophistication

Many people worry about being sophisticated. When they attend a dinner or some other function with people they consider to be their social superiors, they are terrified of being unsophisticated. Well, this should be the least of their worries.

If Webster is still correct, *sophisticated* means "the absence of grossness," it means "worldly wise," "blasé," and experienced in the ways of society. Sophisticated implies refinement, urbanity, cleverness, and cultivation. The word *sophistication* also implies wealth and knowledge.

But, then again, the *same dictionary* defines *sophistication* as "altering deceptively," to adulterate, to deprive of genuineness or simplicity. There are those who don't know the first thing about sophistication but who are considered sophisticated by others when, in reality, they're fakes.

Jesus Christ certainly was wise to the *ways* of the world. He certainly would qualify as one who was *refined*. But would you call him sophisticated? I don't think so, because today's image of sophistication carries a lot of baggage with it. It carries qualities of the show-off, the egotist, the individual so insecure that he must display what he considers smart.

That great philosopher, Jimmy Durante, once addressed the topic of sophistication. He said, "I not only ain't sophisticated, but I can't hardly pronounce the word." And he became beloved and sought after. Durante's advice to anyone who might feel self-conscious was, "Be yourself." If you are dress-ing to please yourself, if you are a pleasant person to be around, if you are a good listener, if you can *be* yourself—you're sophisticated. You don't have to prove it.

Being yourself is the best impression you can make.

Tastes and Desires

*T*here's an old, misleading bromide that says opposites attract. I guess that's possible, but I picked up a study from the University of Southern California that says opposites do *not* attract—in fact, just the opposite.

Men and women who are dating tend to have similar ways of behaving and thinking—when they're "in love." The study shows that the happiest couples are those who are most alike. It would be dangerous to a relationship if one decides the other would be a good catch and fakes interest in what the other person likes.

For example, a man is struck by a woman's good looks. So, in order to try to win her, he decides to go along with her love of concerts, opera, and museums, when, in reality, he'd rather go bowling, drink a few beers with the boys, and play poker. Sooner or later she's going to find out that he doesn't go for *Carmen* or *Cavelaria Rusticanna* and he doesn't know Mozart from Moses—and doesn't care.

Maybe he thinks *she's* so enamored with *him* that pretty soon, *she'll* adapt to *his* likes and life-style. Well, I tried this out on a couple of our church counselors in the premarriage arena, and they seem to think, as do I, that it's a two-way street. *He* can't fake liking her tastes and *she* shouldn't try faking his likes. If *she* feigns interest in bowling, golf, football, tattoos, chugalug, and fast cars, you will eventually have a very unhappy couple who had better know about these things before hiring a caterer.

There are two kinds of honesty involved here. And both are very important—honesty with each other and most important, honesty with *oneself*. That's where so many of us fail. We won't admit why we're doing what we're doing.

Of all the gifts God gives us, one of the greatest is the power to reason. We should use it.

Choosing Your Partner

There's one thing that young single people think about a lot. Probably more than anything else, whether they'll admit it or not. It's finding the right person with whom to spend the rest of their lives.

Interestingly enough, when it comes to that very special someone, looks, power and prestige are pretty far down on the list. I came across a study done by *Parents* magazine and here's what they found out when they asked a thousand Americans what they looked for in the opposite sex.

Most—78 percent—said a person should be *caring* and *considerate*. Trust and honesty fits into this category.

About 60 percent said they looked for someone with a good sense of humor.

Fifty-eight percent said they wanted someone who would share their interests.

Next on the list—and I must mention that this list offered several choices, so answers will add up to more than a hundred—40 percent wanted a good conversationalist, especially one who was intelligent.

Fifty percent wanted a partner who was romantic and physically loving.

About 40 percent said it would be terrific if their person of choice was widely respected.

A third of those in this survey said that their person of choice should be charming. Those who avoided Prince Charming worried about exactly what *charming* meant, and with whom would Prince Charming be charming?

Only 11 percent took looks into consideration, an attractive face or body.

Only 4 percent said they'd want the person to have money. What's important here, I think, is that these answers were anonymous and there was no reason to lie or impress anyone. So all in all, it bodes well for those seeking mates.

Billy Graham said it well: "There are more marriages than divorces...which shows you that preachers still can out-talk lawyers."

A Prayer for
a Young Couple

*O*ne of the writers on my TV show paraphrased a wedding blessing and it made a nice little prayer. I thought I'd share it with you:

Dear Lord, their joys are doubled today. Bless this husband. May his strength be her protection, his character be his pride, and may he so live that she will find in him the haven for which the heart of a woman truly longs.

Bless this loving wife. Give her a tenderness that will make her great, a deep sense of understanding, and a great faith in Thee. Give her that inner beauty of soul that never fades, that eternal youth that is found in holding fast the things that never age.

Teach them that marriage is not merely living for each other; it is two people joining hands to serve You. Give them a great spiritual purpose in life. Let them discover that perfection will not be found in each other, but only in Thee. May they minimize each other's weaknesses, and be swift to praise and magnify each other's good points and strengths. Let them see each other through a lover's kind and patient eyes.

Give them enough tears to keep them tender, enough little hurts to keep them humane, enough failure that they will keep their hands clasped tightly with Thine...but, please Lord, enough success to make them certain they are walking with God.

May they never take each other's love for granted, but keep within them that breathless wonder that says, "Out of all this world you have chosen me." And, dear Lord, when life is done and the sun is setting, may they still stand hand in hand, thanking You for each other, and serve Thee happily, faithfully together until, at last, one shall lay the other in Your arms.

Rules for a Happy Marriage

*T*here is a little flyer that newlyweds can post on the refrigerator door, or, even better, commit to memory. It's called "Rules for a Happy Marriage. The list reads like this:

First, *never both be angry at the same time.* Good rule...and better if you can do it.

Second, *never shout at each other unless the house is on fire.*

Third, *if one of you has to win an argument, let it be your mate.*

Fourth, *if you have to criticize, do it lovingly.*

Fifth, *never bring up mistakes of the past.* To break that rule is to bring on a volatile situation. It's childish to react with a line that goes: "Oh, yeah? How about the time you...."

Sixth, *neglect the whole world rather than each other.* Oh, how many marriages would be saved if that rule were followed.

Seventh, *never go to bed with an argument unsettled.* You may lose a little sleep, but this one works, too.

And—very important—*at least once every day, try to say one kind or complimentary thing to your life's partner.* That isn't difficult to do. Just look and listen a little. When you have done something wrong, be ready to admit it and ask for forgiveness. Remember...it takes two to make a quarrel, and the wrong one is the one who does the most talking.

Love and Marriage

Comedian Alan King said it. "If you want to read about love and marriage, you have to buy two books." Well, it's a good gag. It isn't exactly true, but many people feel that way.

A lot of frustrated people go looking for answers in bookstores. For instance, there's a book titled *Love the Way You Want It* that sets out to dispel some popular romantic myths.

Myth number one: "Living together before marriage will demonstrate whether your marriage will succeed." Actually, this is a myth that needs uncovering. Reliable statistics show that people who live together before marriage are more likely to divorce than are those who wait until they're married.

But this book, by psychologist Robert J. Steinberg, has some other interesting ideas. Dr. Steinberg says it's a myth that "love conquers all." He feels that one person cannot change the other by the sheer force of love. True change and personal growth must come from within.

Then he explodes another myth: "You can tell what kind of a spouse someone will be by considering how they were raised." Of course, you can't. It seems to me that what matters most isn't the experiences a person has had, it's what he or she has learned from them. Many wonderful people have come from disadvantaged or even dysfunctional families.

I've always felt that young couples put a great onus on the word *love*. Love *is* great. It's essential. But love alone can leave a young couple on shaky ground, if their views and expectations of life are mismatched. Love is wonderful—when it's mixed in with understanding, compassion, good cheer, and a lot of patience.

So when you hear, "Love conquers all," you might ask, "Love and what else?"

Kids and Television

From the first day that Kukla, Fran, and Ollie flickered to life on television back in 1948, thousands of people and organized groups and committees have been on television's back. And most of them are still there.

Now we have a new voice being heard, the American Academy of Pediatrics, which says that if youngsters watch too much television, it could cause violently aggressive behavior and obesity. They're saying too much television could turn your baby into a mean, fat kid.

Researchers are now studying the link between TV watching and drug abuse, TV watching and sexual behavior, TV watching and alcoholism, TV and low school grades. I guess the only thing TV isn't being blamed for is hammertoes and plantar's warts.

Here's the academy's summation—or, if you're a critic, too, their indictment:

American kids spend twenty-five hours a week watching TV. By age seventy, they will have spent seven years in front of that television set. Of course, by age seventy they'll be a little more cynical and less impressionable, so, in a way, that boxcar figure is a little capricious. Today's children, the academy says, watch an average of fourteen thousand sexual scenes a year, two thousand beer and wine commercials, and a plethora of suggestive music videos.

Many parents are very concerned. They put the blame squarely on TV programmers. But I rather like what Bob Keeshan had to say about all this. Bob, as you know, held forth as TV's Captain Kangaroo for many years. He said, "You can't use television as a substitute for parenting. *You* have to spend some time with your child."

After all, it is you the parent who creates the strongest image your child will ever remember.

Time for Kids

"Where does the time go?" Well, the answer to that depends on where you're standing.

We adults would like to hoard time. Children can't wait to spend it. For kids, the time spent in school can be an eternity. Time befuddles them. Why does summer go so fast? And why do car trips take so long? No parent will ever escape the plaintive call from the backseat, "How much farther is it?" Or: "Are we there yet?"

Most of childhood is lived in an urgent present tense...and in that state, everything is noticed in terms of "how long?" Their lives are not tarnished with routine yet. They are looking for the new, the next page in their lives.

We tell them to be patient. We admonish them for being so jumpy. We explain that we are older and wiser, and that things don't happen "just like that." We must make haste slowly. Anything worth having is worth working for and waiting for.

When the child's questions cause us to become impatient ourselves, we tend to say, "When I was your age, I..." Or we might answer that trip question with, "No we're not there yet. Go to sleep. I'll wake you up when we get there." And what have we done? We've turned ourselves into our own parents.

There is no doubt—no doubt at all—that children's questions can drive you right up the wall. But remember, they're only asking to smell the flowers. They can't help you with your grown-up problems and anxieties. They are only little voices. And that's your challenge...to try to keep them still and interested with your sagacity and power.

Remember, Jesus said, "Suffer the children..." Not suffer the parents. Show them you're smarter. You'll get more respect.

The Empty Nest

I visited a home last week that was the epitome of neatness. It was spotless. It was quiet. You could hear the clock on the mantel ticking. The chairs around the dining room table were in absolutely perfect alignment.

It wasn't exactly the way I remembered that house from previous visits. Now, don't misunderstand me. I don't have a fetish for neatness, nor do I mind a little messiness...but something was different here. The last time I'd visited the house there were jackets tossed over every chair in the house, ties and blouses hanging from doorknobs, snack dishes piled in the sink and loud rock music pouring from the den.

The reason for the change was obvious. The kids were away at college, and Mother and Dad finally had something they had waiting a long time for. Would the day ever come when Mom wouldn't have to bend over to pick up socks from the landing on the stairs. But thinking back, he remembered the days when he'd bent over to pick up choo-choo trains and rubber balls and toy soldiers...and how he waited for the day when the kids would be big enough to pick up their own toys. She felt like her work wound never end.

Now, all the years of chaos, of laughing and crying and noisy confrontations are nearly gone. Oh, the kids will be home for the holidays...and it looks like a marriage down the road for one of them. . .and they certainly have become respectable adults—messy, but respectable. And now there is the peace and the quiet. Everything stays right where they put it. They can watch anything they want on television. . .or even nothing at all.

A tacit sigh is there now. . .and they wonder, those noisy, crazy, wild days when the kids were growing up. . .were they the days we were supposed to smell the flowers?

Of course they were. And the kids. They were the flowers. They always will be.

Letting Go

*H*ow many young mothers weep when they put their firstborn on the school bus to take that first ride into the care of someone else? And how many fathers give a leery look at the first young man who comes to call on a teenage daughter?

While mothers and fathers look happily down the road to when their children will be grown, educated, and living life on their own, the process of letting go is heart-wrenching. Mothers and fathers tend to think of it as an ending. A loss. But it isn't.

Letting go doesn't mean to stop caring. It only means that someone else will share your care. Ah! That's the hard part. Letting go doesn't mean to cut yourself off. The one you are letting go will need your support now more than ever. You will help that boy or girl guide themselves through adventures they've never experienced before. But if you don't let go, they'll never learn the things they *have* to learn in order to survive. To let go is to learn you don't have to care *for*. . . but care *about*. To let go is not to deny, but to accept.

You must learn that letting go is not being in the middle of everything arranging all the outcomes. Letting go only means that more people will be coming into your life. Your circle of friends will be greater, you will learn a lot more about the world around you. You will learn not to judge but to allow another to be a human being. You will remember your own young desires to be your own person, and you will accept the fact that your offspring are no longer bewildering—only human, like you.

To let go is not to regret the past, but to grow— and live for the future. Because once you really let go, you will find a future that can be so beautiful, so full of adventure and love that it will nearly overwhelm you.

Charlie and the Church

A ny priest or minister can tell you that we see many people at church on Easter Sunday and at Midnight Mass on Christmas Eve whom we never see at any other time of the year.

In many homes, it's a kind of a family joke. "When Charlie goes to church, the walls shake." This is the same Charlie who loves his wife and children dearly and is very concerned about the decline in church attendance and is very upset about the closing of private schools for lack of funding. Charlie is really a very nice guy—and will gladly show you his baptismal certificate. He got that in church. His marriage license is in his safety deposit box. He had that signed in the church in which he was married—the church he now attends twice a year or so. Every one of his daughters will be married in his church—which will bring Charlie's attendance rate up to three or four times in a given year.

As the years pass by, he will weep in his church for the passing of a loved one...perhaps even one of his own. And Charlie often fantasizes and frets about his own funeral in that church. Of course, he never tells anybody about these worries. Will the boys from the fire department be there? Will the aging monsignor still be around, or will one of the younger priests handle his last rites?

Every really important event in Charlie's life has its beginning and will end in Charlie's church. Yet

I wonder if Charlie knows that the doors of his church are *always* open. That he can slip into his church for a quick prayer on the way to work. Or after work. I guess inertia sets in as the years go by.

But—even if it's just for the look of it—Charlie would notice lots of smiles if, when his wife and daughters slide into the pew, he was right behind them.

Father Le Jacq

You don't know him; you'll probably never meet him. But I'd like to tell you about a Maryknoll priest and doctor who, after his ordination in 1987, found himself engulfed in an AIDS epidemic that was surfacing worldwide. Today he's working in a hospital in Tanzania.

In the area around him, over one hundred thousand children have lost at least one parent to AIDS. Another ten thousand have lost both parents. His hospital serves regional referrals for six million people in the Lake Victoria area. Father Peter Le Jacq maintains a double vocation—priest *and* doctor.

African hospitals are ill-equipped for the growing number of AIDS patients, and Father Le Jacq realized that the only way he was going to make any headway against this disease was to come up with a comprehensive program that included not only treatment, but home care, pastoral ministry, and, above all, an education program for the general public to help *prevent* the spread of AIDS.

So Father Le Jacq, with less than a handful of associates, started a campaign for all primary and secondary schools in the Mwanza District—using charts and graphs and videos, anything to get the message across. He stresses to these children without parents that the prevention of AIDS is best assured by the monogamous life.

What makes this tall, lanky, soft-spoken, missionary-doctor my candidate for sainthood is that rather than live a life of ease and popularity among his peers elsewhere, he has chosen to work among the thousands of dying to help save the living, and steer their children away from a hellish death.

When Pope John Paul II visited Africa in 1990, the Tanzanian bishops asked Father Le Jacq to brief the pope on the AIDS situation. The Pope listened carefully and expressed grave concern. He said "You are doing a difficult job. I will pray for you."

And so will we.

NASA's Most Respected Scientist

This is a very short story about America's leading scientist in the search for life in outer space. He is probably the most respected scientist at NASA— the National Aeronautics and Space Administration. These are the people who put men and women in orbit, who send up the space shuttle to do chores in outer space.

His name is Kent Cullers, and when he was only 25, he wrote a computer program showing that a radar system NASA planned to install in the space shuttle wasn't cost-efficient. NASA was so impressed that they hired him.

His project these days is to help NASA in its search for E.I.—extraterrestrial intelligence. In October 1992, on the 500th anniversary of the discovery of America by Columbus, the agency began the biggest radio-telescope search in history. In sixty seconds, NASA can investigate more possibilities than all the searches ever conducted in the history of space. Kent Cullers's job is to sift through all the radio noise and seek out signs of intelligent communications from space. His machinery is so efficient, it could scan the entire *Encyclopedia Brittanica* in one second.

When Kent's wife was about to deliver their first baby, the air conditioner in the hospital room quit. The monitor tracking the baby's heartbeat malfunctioned. . .and Ken Cullers coolly wiped his wife's brow with one hand and with the other worked on the hot cord dangling from the machine. A nurse, in panic, rushed into the room and shouted, "You can't fool with that machine!" "It's okay," Kent said. "I'm a physicist with NASA."

There's one thing I haven't told you about this tall, handsome man: Kent Cullers is blind, has been since he was born. As a young boy he wrote—in block letters in a note book: "God is great. But so am I."

Patricia Neal's Burden

She's over sixty; she's still beautiful; she's a lively conversationalist; she's starred in some of Hollywood's greatest movies, opposite some of Hollywood's most popular leading men. Her name: Patricia Neal. She was on top, had everything to live for. She was on Easy Street.

Then a series of tragedies stalked Patricia Neal. Her firstborn son was hit by a car and run over in his carriage. The baby sustained serious brain damage. Then Patricia Neal's younger daughter came down with a serious illness—one that almost took her life. Patricia Neal kept on working; she felt she had to. She was living with tragedy over which she had no control.

Her next great success was in the movie *Hud*, with Paul Newman, but right after filming was over she suffered a devastating stroke. Very few of her friends expected her to survive, let alone recover. But she had a tremendous will to live, and she was surrounded by family and friends who worked tirelessly for months to help her regain what she once had. She did respond and finally was able enough to do another picture. This time, *The Subject Was Roses*. Then shortly afterward, her husband left her to marry her best friend.

Today, though, there's no bitterness. In fact, Patricia is quite understanding about the forces that would have broken another woman. She dedicates herself to her family. She understands the stress her husband must have felt during her long recovery period. Although she walks with a slight limp, she doesn't feel sorry for herself. She says she's looking forward to her next adventure.

Patricia Neal is a great reminder that self-pity and bitterness simply get in the way of a happy life. We can learn a lesson from her—and all the others like her that we meet: If we nurse our angers and sorrows, we have no energy left for living.

Mother Teresa

No one in recent times has so personified the work of our Lord as has Mother Teresa of Calcutta. There have been books written about her works among the sick and the poor—and more books will be written.

I had the great good fortune to have met and worked with this saintly person during her visit to America; and you would have to see her, be with her, talk with her, and watch her to appreciate the aura that surrounds this woman.

If you did, you would wonder why...why this aging woman who has done so much for so many, this woman, who, herself, suffers pain—why Mother Teresa doesn't just accept her accolades and step out of her humble role.

Here is how she answers that: "We must not drift away from the humble works, because these are the works nobody will do. It is never too small. *We* are so small we look at things in a small way. But God, being almighty, sees everything great. Even if you write a letter for a blind man, or you just go and sit and listen, or you take the mail for them, or you visit somebody—or bring a flower to somebody—small things—or wash clothes for somebody or clean house."

"Very humble work," Mother Teresa says, "*that* is where you and I must be. For there are many people who can do big things. But there are very few people who will do the small things. It is the small things that sisters and brothers do. We can do very little for the people, but at least they know that we do love them and that we care for them and that we are at their disposal."

If Mother Teresa taught me anything after all my training for the priesthood, it's that small things are truly big things through a different set of eyes. Any of us who ever felt humble, could still take a lesson from Mother Teresa. Remember the "little things."

In Defense of Messiness

I've found an author who has been able to demolish a few long-entrenched myths about the workplace. Example: "A messy desk indicates a careless, unproductive slob." (I sure hope not! You should see mine sometimes.)

Ann McGee Cooper has written a book titled *You Don't Have to Go Home Exhausted*, in which she says a cluttered desk usually indicates a person who thrives on jumping back and forth from project to project and enjoys the stimulus of seeing his work in progress. I'll go along with that.

Another myth is that "We all need seven to eight hours of sleep per night." No, she says. Brief naps during the workday can restore energy for many people who sleep only four or five hours a night. At least, that's what you tell the boss when you're caught napping on the job.

It's also important to balance work and play. Take a short break during your workday and forget work altogether for a few minutes. And watch out for the dangerous "p" word—*perfectionism*. Perfectionism will give you stomach pains and high blood pressure—just like it did to your perfectionist boss. So, don't *be* like the boss. Live a little. Indeed, Cooper says, the biggest mistake adults make is to turn work into work. It should be challenging, productive—*and* fun. Just being busy doesn't count.

As the French novelist, André Gide, put it, "Each moment becomes an anxiety in my brain. I am becoming the ugliest of all things—a busy man." Of course, that was his kind of humor. But remember that even the Lord Himself took time out for meditation and quiet periods during His ministry.

So. . .there is no admonishment for a messy desk. It's not even a venial sin.

Who Prays?

*I*f you were to judge by the media coverage, there are a lot of people who pray and a lot of people who not only don't pray, but don't believe in it and don't want other people to pray...especially in public.

Recently, a study conducted by Andrew Greeley, a best-selling author, asked fifteen hundred Americans, "Do you pray?"

Now, these fifteen hundred were not all church-goers or synagogue-goers, but, amazingly enough, only 1 percent of the fifteen hundred interviewed said they never prayed—1 percent. Fifty-seven percent said they prayed every day, and 78 percent said they prayed once a week—78 percent! That's a larger majority than voted in the biggest presidential landslide.

It was that 78 percent Geeley found intriguing. He asked, "How can one explain such frequency of prayers, not only among those who believe in God and life after death, but especially among those who do not believe in God or survival? Do they address their prayers to "To Whom it May Concern?"

Father Greeley said he wasn't quite sure why prayer is so pervasive. This is an area of human behavior that could use a lot more exploration.

Some interesting sidebars to this study: Americans and Irish were among the most prayerful people. Both had an 80-percent prayer rate. The prayer rate in Italy and Spain was 70 percent. The British came in at 50 percent, with the French right behind at 45 percent.

Not bad for a skeptical world. Let us pray.

Homelessness

"*F*oxes have dens and birds of the sky have nests, but the Son of Man has nowhere to rest his head." A rather astonishing line. It's from Luke 9:58.

Well, you might say, that was then and this is now, and I live in a house with a furnace and air-conditioning and three bedrooms. If so, you're one of the lucky ones. In almost every community, and certainly in every large metropolitan center, there are more homeless people than anyone wants to hear about. Even Jesus knew the anguish of having no place to sleep, and He warns the potential follower not to follow Him seeking comfort or success.

Being without a place to sleep in comfort is not the *only* kind of homelessness. Let's take the multi-millionaire, the mogul with the biggest house on the hill, with five cars in the driveway, the Olympic-size pool, and three tennis courts. He's happy to point out that there is a working fireplace in each of the nine bedrooms and that the carpeting was especially woven for him in India.

But you can be homeless in a castle. Unless this man understands a simple principle of the Holy Word, he is, in truth, homeless. Regardless of how many bedrooms and how many fireplaces...no matter how large the pool or how many cars are in the driveway...they'll be of absolutely no consequence when the owner leaves it all for eternity.

We are homeless when we are so far from God that we can't find our way back. We are homeless when we forget that our true home is in the next world: the home to which God calls each of us.

The Instant
of Understanding

*I*n his book, *The Jesus Effect*, Dr. Dennis Hensley talks about instant understanding and uses some examples to explain what it is.

As a youngster, he recalls, he and his little buddies played War. Most boys do. The rules were simple: If you got "shot," you fell down and counted to sixty before you could get up again.

Years later he was in a *real* army, carrying a *real* rifle through the *real* jungles of Vietnam. He had been through basic training and was told how things would be, but as he crouched in the heavy foliage, suddenly the tree branches and the large fronds above him were shredded into a thousand pieces of leaf pulp as enemy machine guns riddled his position. He dropped to his knees, he says, and went white with terror.

He realized he could have been killed right then and there. "Hey! This isn't 'count to sixty and get up.' This is real war." It was a highly dramatic moment of comprehension. An *instant* of *understanding*.

He also recalls a more peaceful, but equally astonishing instant. After a couple of years of marriage, his wife told him that a baby was on the way. He was happy. That was nice. But three months later, when his wife put his hand on her stomach, and he actually felt the baby kick—that's when it registered. "Wow!" he said. "Now I really understand that a real human being is on its way."

The Bible tells of many personal confrontations that became instants of understanding. Such as what happened to Peter when Jesus, after the Resurrection, asked him three times, "Do you love me?" And Peter answered, "You know that I love you." At that moment when Peter realized that Jesus could forgive his denials and still love him, Peter's life was changed forever.

It's so true that our lives can be changed in an instant...an instant when we comprehend the wonders of God.

The Gift of Laughter

A young couple I know—newlyweds—told me they have a very difficult time when they argue. "We just get going, trying to outshout each other, and suddenly we realize how ridiculous the whole thing is, and how stupid we look and sound, and we break down in uncontrollable laughter. We just can't stop laughing. We're hysterical. And it makes fighting extremely difficult."

Well, this couple has something very precious. The gift of laughter. It's too bad we all don't have it. Laughter can do some amazing things. It's God's perfect tension breaker. And we humans are the only species blessed with this gift.

Laughter can help us put things in perspective. Any successful comedian knows that the biggest laughs come from an audience that relates to the material. It's like the couple who realize how ridiculous they look fighting. They recognize the futility and find it funny. Recognition. Laughter.

Actually, though, *God* gave us the *ability* to laugh. There is a time for laughter because we are all, to one degree or another, poets. Many professional comedians and innumerable philosophers have tried to make a clinical study of laughter because it is unique with us, and because understanding it would be a boon to anyone who makes a living telling jokes.

With laughter comes relief. When the famous author and editor Norman Cousins found himself with a serious nerve disorder that was diagnosed as life-threatening, he rented a hotel suite and bought every silly movie comedy around, and, according to his own testimony, literally laughed himself back to good health. He laughed at the Marx Brothers, W. C. Fields, Bob Hope, Charlie Chaplin . . . anybody he found funny.

But we can't isolate laughter any more than we can clinically define agony and tears. I believe God gave us laughter as a subtle safety valve for our struggles.

Despair whispers, "Life has no meaning." Laughter says, "You're wrong. Life is a joy." We can cope better once we reduce stress—and a good laugh helps us do that.

So don't be afraid to laugh. It frees the heart. It puts things in perspective. It's God's gift.

The Scorpion's Alibi

Jack Paar—who once was the king of late-night TV—said, "If you want a lot of real trouble, just do somebody a favor." It's only natural to feel that way sometimes, when people we try to help keep pushing us beyond reasonable requests.

I'm reminded of the fable about the beaver and the scorpion. The scorpion asked the beaver if he could ride across the river on the beaver's back. The beaver said, "I can't let you ride on my back. You'd sting me and kill me." The scorpion said, "No I wouldn't. If I can't get across the river, I'll be killed myself. And if I try to swim, I'll drown. Why would I want to kill someone who'd be so kind to me?" So the beaver said, "Okay. Jump on my back." And the scorpion rode across the river.

When they got to the other side, the scorpion stung the beaver . . . and as the beaver was dying, he asked, "Why did you do that? You promised not to sting me if I took you across the river." And the scorpion said, "I'm sorry, I can't help it. It's my nature."

Now let's translate that to human beings. First of all, we are not scorpions—although some humans may act as if they were. Humans are capable of controlling their instinctive tendencies. Humans can change their way of thinking because humans can think.

Many people say, "I'm sorry I did that, but it's just my nature. I can't help it." When you have hurt another human with words or deeds—when you cause any kind of harm—the excuse that "it's just my nature" doesn't work. It will never work, because you are God's person, and it is not your "nature" to hurt or kill—to ruin a life. You know better.

Psalm 34:14 says, "Keep your tongue from evil and your lips from speaking guile; turn from evil, and do good; seek peace, and follow after it." And in 2 Peter 2:11 we read: "Keep away from worldly desires that wage war against the soul."

Plainly put. Easy to learn...sometimes hard to do.

Two Smiles Make Three

Every once in a while, we sit quietly for a moment at night and think, *I've really had a good day today.* Most of us do it all too seldom, because it seems that wherever we look, whatever we do, whatever we hope to do, there's something or someone who makes life a little bit more difficult. And I fear it will be that way until we meet our Maker.

It really doesn't take much to "make someday's day." Maybe it's just a smile. A pat on the back. Perhaps it's just withholding criticism for once. It's amazing to me that more people aren't able to smile readily. Technically it's harder on your face to frown. We're told a frown utilizes twice as many muscles as a smile does.

There is the smiler and the "smiled at." When someone gives you a warm, genuine smile, don't you just want to share it? And when you do, you start a ripple effect. Tensions ease. A little bit of stress is lifted. If you look about you in the course of an ordinary day, you notice that those people with the nastiest disposition are the most stressed-out. It's actually very hard on the body to be unpleasant. If affects just about everything inside—including the digestive system, the stomach, the eyes, the joints, and—especially—the brain.

It's very easy for me to quote the old saw, "Smile and the world smiles with you, cry and you cry alone," but crying won't make your day. There are things that happen to us, things that people do to

us that seem rude, uncaring, and even hateful—
and heaving a sigh and smiling to yourself is very,
very difficult (but not impossible).

You will be surprised at how many really good
things will happen to you, how many compliments
will be returned, if you just look for something nice
to say and give somebody—anybody—some little
thing to smile about.

Too Many Choices

Watching the long lines of people in Russia waiting in front of grocery shelves that have no groceries, and remembering that even under the Communists, the people of Moscow had so very few choices made me think how we, here in the United States, have a fantastic array of items to pick from.

Americans can choose from more than twenty-five thousand items in supermarkets. We can choose from scores of models of cars, TV sets, VCRs and CDs. If you have cable, you can choose from—at least—36 program channels. There are nearly eleven thousand magazines or periodicals available. There's something for everyone in America whatever your tastes or needs.

Maybe the marketing geniuses are outsmarting themselves. Some experts say that Americans are becoming overwhelmed—even paralyzed—by all these choices and that apathy is spilling over into other areas of our lives. The psychologists are saying that all these choices don't make our lives easier. They tend to stifle us...and we become more anxious.

The average American has to make literally hundreds of conscious and unconscious decisions every day. And when you should be calm and full of the expectation of enjoyment, you're getting yourself all worked up. In his book, *Future Shock*, Alvin Toffler said that reaction time slows down as the number of choices increases. If you have an infinite number of choices, you can be reduced to passivity.

It would be a good idea for everyone to forgo the choices for an hour or so, and go to a place where the choices are fewer, and the experience is calming.

How about church?

Envy—The Deadly Sin

One of the least talked about—one of the least-admitted—vices is that of envy. Psychiatrists, neurologists, and family doctors can't detect it easily, and yet it can cause emotional and physical disturbances that can literally destroy people. The rather amazing thing about it is that people who are good in every other way can harbor deep-seated envy.

In America, it manifests itself in a very puzzling way—and, believe it or not, the media have a lot to do with this. A movie actor, a rock singer, an athlete, a politician comes from ground zero—and suddenly there's a media hype for this underdog. Then the star rises, and when popularity—or notoriety—reaches its peak—the game is to shoot him down. This eases the envy syndrome built up in the reader or viewer. It truly *is* a media game.

In our personal lives we wonder why it is that others seem to be more favored than we are by God and the circumstances of life. The problem is intensified if we see someone who does not seem to be a particularly good person prospering and enjoying comfort and security. It can even hurt to hear someone else praised, especially if we think that maybe *we* deserve a little praise once in a while.

The brothers of Joseph were guilty of envy. They were saddened and very angry because of the favors Joseph received, and they looked at his good fortune as a threat to them.

Of course, envy is born of pride and selfishness. We all recognize and have seen the line from Genesis 37:4: "When his brothers saw that their father loved him best of all his sons, they hated him so much that they would not even greet him."

Recognize envy for what it is. A vice. A sin. And you'll probably be better able to handle it.

The Game of Avarice, Envy, and Spite

*I*n 2 Peter 2:10, 13, 14 we read about some pretty sinful people. They're "bold and arrogant" and "not afraid to revile glorious beings. . ." They think "daytime revelry a delight; they are stains and defilements. . .Their eyes are full of adultery and insatiable for sin. They seduce unsteady people, and their hearts are trained in greed."

Who are these people? Well, there's a new board game called "Let's Buy Hollywood" that rewards such enduring human qualities as raw ambition, malice, envy, and spite. To say nothing of avarice. So they might be the ancestors of the game people.

This game differs from most Hollywood games because it concerns itself with the *business* side of movies instead of the stars. The players must assemble talent packages that include an actor, actress, screenwriter, and director and then make a movie and put it into distribution to generate revenue. You can build an entertainment empire that includes television stations, theater chains, and a cable network.

Now, the wheeling and dealing comes with forming alliances with other players to buy out and destroy someone else, to cause other properties to come tumbling down. Here's where one's ability at deception and raiding is tested.

But as funny as this idea is, things are not all peaches and cream for "Let's Buy Hollywood." Cathy Rubin, the inventor, says it's not for the emotionally fragile. "The person who says he loves it," she says, "is the person who won yesterday. Even when I've played in a group and lost, I'd be in a bad mood for the rest of the night and the next day."

Well, I believe in free enterprise and wish the inventor well, but there's something about even *playing* the game of avarice, envy, greed, and spite that can be depressing. It's too much like real life.

The Profit Takers

I nvestigative reporters who specialize in economics have been digging into the problems of the nation's economy, and they seem to think the problems started in the eighties when there was a rampage of leveraged buyouts in which companies were taken over by other companies, stripped of their assets and sold again with the wheeler-dealers pocketing huge profits rather than reinvesting money into the properties they acquired.

These buyouts and sellouts cost hundreds of thousands of jobs and sent a chill of anxiety all through the American job market. The blame, they say, should be laid at the feet of the profit-takers. Others blame a Congress that makes it possible. But the primary beast is called Greed.

In *Meditations with Dante Alighieri* we read:

> The terrifying beasts that confronted me were the leopard of lust, the lion of pride, and the wolf of greed, who was the fiercest of the three. The wolf of greed is so vicious and perverse that it never satisfies its greedy desires—and, after feeding, is hungrier than before. Many are the beasts with which it mates, and there will yet be more until the Hound, the Holy Spirit, shall come and deal it a painful death. He will not feed on land or money, but on wisdom, love and strength. This Savior will hunt it through every town until God has driven it back to hell, whence envy first set it forth.

So, you see, greed of great magnitude is nothing new. The advice of Jesus is, "If you wish to be perfect, go and sell what you own and give the money to the poor; then come, follow me." One thing is certain. True happiness is found in giving, not taking.

The Age of Affluence

I guess the public relations people feel that the best thing you can do during a serious recession is remind people how well-off they are. This is a perfectly normal bureaucratic reaction, but the list of American assets is rather interesting.

A study from Tweak Marketing found that more Americans own television sets than own bathtubs. They own more television sets than telephones. Ninety-eight percent of all American homes have at least one TV set—and nearly half the homes have more than one. Eighty percent now have a microwave oven. Eighty percent! And, 71 percent of all Americans own a still camera. Sixty-four percent have a VCR. Half of all American homes have dishwashers. Eighteen percent have home computers.

If material possessions indicate affluence, then we might be fairly affluent. Except...television sets don't guarantee job security, and dishwashers don't avert corporation downsizing and loss of jobs. And microwave ovens don't prevent family arguments.

It's hard to believe that there was a time when nobody had any of these things. Not that homelife used to be better or easier, but today there seems to be some indication that we are spoiling ourselves. Instead of involving ourselves in doing what's good for us—instead of exercising, instead of writing those letters, instead of making those phone calls, instead of paying those visits—it's so easy just to put our feet up and click away at those 36 television channels we now have available to us.

Americans seem to feel that distraction is an important part of life. We work very hard at being amused and forgetting. To a point where many of us forget what we were trying to forget. Here's something to remember—from 2 Corinthians 9:8, "God is able to make every grace abundant for you, so that in all things...you may have an abundance for every good work."

I would add: "So don't make that armchair your second home."

Success Is Not a Sin

"*T*ake care to guard against all greed, for though one may be rich, one's life does not consist of possessions" (Luke 12:14). This is probably the most ignored line in all of the teachings of the Bible.

At the bottom of almost every economic crisis of any nation we find the dreaded "G" word. Greed. It brought down the S & L's and left us with an obscene debt. Throughout recorded history, greed has been the main factor in the ruination of many a civilization. It's a subtle but real temptation. Too many people equate success with possessions. But these are really two different things.

In "Fiddler on the Roof," Tevye, the father, burdened and poverty-stricken, says, "Being poor is no great sin. But it's no great honor, either." I always liked that line. In his own way, Tevye found success in life. He found respect and love.

Saint Luke wrote a great deal about wealth and its dangers. He's the only evangelist who mentions that poor shepherds were the first to learn about the birth of Jesus. Now the Scriptures do not condemn success itself. It is not a sin to work and succeed. God gave us intelligence to use to survive, persevere, and perhaps prosper. We were given the capability to love and care and to appreciate justice and peace. These are the qualities that should sustain us.

Our possessions, however, should not be the badge of our success. The way you act toward other people, the compassion you show for the less fortunate, and the desire always to be of service should be the qualities that people point to when your name is mentioned.

True, many may be awed and envious of what you own; but that's not enough to guarantee they like you—let alone love you.

Self-Esteem

*T*here's a very popular hypothesis in the world of psychology that goes, "In order for you to get people to like you, you have to like yourself first." You don't have to fall in love with yourself, just have the feeling that you're okay.

This all starts with the way you look at things. You watch important people on television—the movers and the shakers. You read about the famous, the adored, the movie stars and beautiful people, and you wish you could emulate them. You feel insecure when you can't. But I believe that we all have talents and a specific role to play on this earth.

You are, here and now, in a place and time that no one else can affect in the same way you can.

Just think of all the little decisions you've made—decisions that affect many lives. Do you have a child? That child wouldn't be here without you. You've already changed this and many generations to come. Have you ever moved? Changed jobs? Helped someone else? Done any of the little things you consider merely normal?

When you think about it, you're a very important person. So important that you've already affected the lives of everyone about you...and you will affect the lives of people you haven't even met yet. The only things that can deter you are self-doubt, complacency, and fear. These emotions are all mixed up with some general misconceptions about yourself. You are you—and there's only one "you."

If you fear rejection, if you are besieged with self-doubt, if you wonder what you will say at an important time in your life—think of what the Bible says in Matthew 10:19, 20: "You will be given at that moment what you are to say. For it will not be you who speak but the Spirit of your Father speaking through you."

The Spiritual Diet

Aside from bibles and cookbooks, there are probably more diet books sold today than any other kind of nonfiction and, if sales are any indication, two-thirds of the country's population are on diets. There's the water diet, the grapefruit diet, the prune juice diet, even the drinking man's diet.

Many of these diets are considered "fad diets." Our obsession with obesity is obvious. I did hear about one book that makes sense to me. It's called *The Love Powered Diet*, by Victoria Moran, who began dieting at age three. She says she was a "fat little girl in a fat-phobic family. My father was a doctor and my mother ran a reducing salon...and I was bad for business."

For years she was tremendously overweight. She dieted, but her weight went up and down until she decided that her philosophy was all wrong. Victoria stopped regarding dieting as a test of willpower. She says, "If you pick up most diet books, the message is, 'You're bad. You have sinned, but if you do what we tell you, you'll lose weight.'"

So Victoria took the sin out of dieting and decided that if dieters love themselves, they'll reward themselves with more healthful food choices. She talks about love-powered food; about walking meditation; about loving the way she now looks—she weighs in at a svelte 116 pounds.

She says that people don't have to embark on an all-or-nothing vegetarian diet. Instead, she advocates positive affirmations—and trying to avoid negative patterns. Your body is you. Love it. Victoria says, "Love is always there. And it's closer than the refrigerator."

The reason I was so taken with this idea is that, as a priest, I've found that true love almost always finds a way.

That Light Under the Bushel

*I*n Luke 11:33 we read, "No one who lights a lamp hides it away or places it [under a bushel basket], but on a lampstand so that those who enter might see the light."

Occasionally we hear about a man or woman who lived like a mole, ate leftover cold food, dressed in rags, and died leaving hundreds of thousands of dollars. Or the writer who drowned his God-given talents in alcohol. We can feel sorry for these people, suspecting that there are mental problems. And there are people who have special talents and find great joy in expressing them—but are cautious and afraid, or not sure what their talents are.

To find your talents, think in terms of what you enjoy doing most. This is often a clue to where talent is buried. Do you like to work with flowers? Then do arrangements for friends and parties. Do you like to write? Then write. Never mind if you have a few critics. If you like to write stories, do it. If poetry is your thing, hop to it. If you simply enjoy organizing things, join a club, join a church, put yourself in a position where your organizational talents are easily recognized.

Talents are not restricted to musical instruments, acting ability, or vocal range. There are talented cooks and bakers, talented conversationalists, and people with the greatest talent of all—the ability to put other people at ease and to be a good friend.

If you are blessed with a skill, don't hoard it. Whatever special qualities or skills we have are gifts from God. And they come with a responsibility to use them well and to make this a better place.

So don't hide your light. Let it shine.

The Dream

The work is anonymous; it's been around for a long time. Nobody seems to know where it came from. But it makes such a perfect moment, I thought I'd include it here:

One night a man had a dream. He dreamed he was walking along the beach with the Lord. Across the sky flashed scenes from his life. For each scene, he noticed two sets of footprints in the sand. One set of prints belonged to him, and the other set of prints belonged to the Lord. When the last scene had flashed before him, he looked back at the footprints and noticed that many times along the path there was only one set of prints in the sand. He also noticed that this happened during the lowest and saddest times in his life.

This really bothered him and he questioned the Lord. "Lord, you said that once I decided to follow you, you would walk all the way with me. But I noticed during the most troublesome times of my life there were only one set of footprints in the sand. I don't understand. Why? Why, when I needed you most—you deserted me."

The Lord replied, "My precious child, I love you and I would never leave you. During the times of trial and suffering, when you saw only one set of prints, it was then that I *carried* you."

When recalling some very difficult, nightmarish time in your life, have you ever found yourself saying, "I don't know how I ever got through it. But somehow, I did." This, of course is a tribute to your inner strength...but inner strength cannot be measured like your height or your weight or your IQ. It can be measured only by how you walk with the Lord.

The End of the Century

I was amazed to learn that the Waldorf Astoria Hotel in New York was already turning down reservations for the New Year's Eve celebration in 1999. So is the Mariott Marquis. This, of course, is supposedly the night that 1999 turns into the year 2000. Whether that's mathematically correct or not is in some dispute, but The World Future Society says that it's like watching the odometer of your car turn over. People get excited.

Then there are the mathematical purists who say we should wait until January 1, 2001. But going from 1999 to 2000 in one evening is a lot more promotable than going from 2000 to 2001. It makes for a nice, big, international party—right or wrong.

Actually, it doesn't really make any difference. The world is older than two thousand years by a couple of billion. A year. . . a hundred years. . . is a speck in time. What God created here is timeless, and if hotels and restaurants want to celebrate our existence on New Year's Eve—and it's good for business—I see no harm.

When you think about it, the whole calendar we use to count days and years is a man-made calculation. As the argument rages as to whether it's 1999, 2000, or 2001, we might reflect on how little time we have here, whatever calendar we go by. How little time and how much we have to do. . . how many things we have to set straight, because when we're ready to enter eternity, calendars don't count.

But if you insist on being mathematically correct about the time frame as the century date changes, look to the banks and airlines. Whatever the banks and airlines *say* it is...it *is*.

As for our mortality—God has His own calendar.

Trees

"*I* think that I shall never see—a poem lovely as a tree." Joyce Kilmer, the man who wrote that line, died in World War I, yet this little poetic essay lives on. What's interesting is that even in these modern times, we don't really know much about trees, except that when they get old, the village workers come and cut them down.

Chemical ecologists from the University of Washington, where trees abound, have discovered that trees have feelings. That's right. Trees have feelings. Trees also have a sex life. These scientists have discovered that trees send unseen signals to other trees. For example, when willows are attacked by webworms and tent caterpillars, they give off a chemical that alerts nearby willows. The other trees respond by pumping more tannin into their leaves, making them more difficult for insects to digest. These researchers found similar responses in maples and birches and other trees.

Scientists have also found that trees respond differently to different attackers. Some trees won't react when their leaves are nipped with sterilized scissors, but they release a venom if they're attacked by an insect.

Trees have made an alliance with nature that we are only beginning to understand. We know about the practical value of trees for everything from medicine to keeping our planet from becoming a desert. . .and yet they seem to have no place in the hearts of twentieth-century real-estate developers.

Wouldn't it be awful if someday we discovered that when we chop down a tree, it screams with pain, but we can't hear it?

A tree is more than just a tree. It's another one of God's mysterious wonders. Joyce Kilmer was so right. "Poems are made by fools like me—but only God can make a tree."

On Being Single

*I*f you remember Paddy Cheyefsky's classic TV play—and movie later—called "Marty," you'll recall the anguish Marty's mother felt when it looked like Marty would never find a nice girl and get married.

Even today, many parents worry and suffer when a son or daughter reaches 25 or 30 and hasn't found someone with whom to settle down. And the young people themselves are sometimes anguished because they feel they're failing somehow.

I found a book that may offer some practical advice instead of solace. It's *The Joy of Being Single* by Janice Harayda. She says single people should think positively. You're doing it alone, she says. And you couldn't have gotten as far as you have without some real accomplishments.

Here are some tips for singles who are in their thirties or forties: Have a life outside the office. Don't marry your job. Keep learning new things. Take up something you couldn't take up if you had other obligations—figure skating, Spanish, French, or a writing course. Don't keep looking back. Don't live in the past or in the future. Don't wear a black arm band for a dead romance. Put down physical roots. Make a home for yourself. Singles need to come home to a place they like. Keep children in your life. And don't shun the opposite sex. Keep them nearby. It's possible to have men or women around without becoming involved.

There's something else she brings up that very few people ever consider—or even think about. But it's there. If you are single, be aware that some married couples can be jealous. Married friends may think you are unhappy, but deep down many of them really envy you.

U.S. Census statistics show that more and more mature women are living successfully alone. By choice...in record numbers. They're busy, they're happy, and another stigma bites the dust.

A Trumpeting
unto the Lord

*R*ecently, at a live television performance of the New York Philharmonic Symphony orchestra, the spotlights played on the principal trumpet of the famous orchestra. He is probably the finest classic trumpeter in the world. He's a bright but modest young man named Philip Smith.

Smith began playing his trumpet in public at services held by the Salvation Army. His father was bandmaster of the Army staff band, and with much scrimping and saving— and a lot of praying—Derek Smith was able to send his son Philip to the Juilliard School in Manhattan.

Young Philip was as intent as he was talented, and after graduation, he was signed by the Chicago Symphony, but his eye had always been on that lead trumpet chair with the New York Philharmonic— then under the direction of Leonard Bernstein.

Two things, he feels, helped him toward his goal. Of course, there was his love and dedication to his craft that echoed his father's hopes for him—but there was something else. His firm belief in the goodness of God and his tireless work for the betterment of humanity—as mandated by the Salvation Army.

How does young Philip Smith handle his new-found fame and the accolades poured upon him by classical music lovers, and the people who buy his albums? Well, next Christmas he'll be exactly where he was last Christmas—in his Salvation Army uniform, outside a department store here and a supermarket there, playing carols, hour after hour, his golden trumpet urging shoppers to drop a little change into the Salvation Army kettle. His cap will be pulled down tight, and the teenagers will tease him, and not a soul will know that it would be impossible for them to get tickets to hear Philip Smith play at Avery Fisher Hall.

And "Silent Night" will never sound so good.

Emily Post's Legacy

*F*or those who never heard of Emily Post, she was the first and last word on etiquette since 1922. Her words on human behavior set a standard for manners and decorum.

Here are some of Emily Post's answers to questions that anxious readers asked those many years ago: "Fashionable ladies never take off their hats." Even the hostess herself wears a hat at a formal luncheon in her own house. What about gloves and face veils? Well, you never wear gloves while eating —and never carry food under or behind a face veil. Then there was the question about guests who overstay their welcome. I quote, "You can provide for that contingency by instructing your butler or waitress to tell her when her car is at the door."

Miss Post also had advice to train travelers. "On a railroad train, you should be careful not to assail the nostrils of fellow passengers with strong odors of any kind. There is a combination of banana and the leather-smell of a valise containing food that is, to many people, emetic."

And in 1922, Emily Post admonished: "A gentleman does not bow to a lady from a club window. Ladies must never be discussed in a men's club. A born gentleman avoids the mention of names exactly as he avoids the mention of how much things cost. Both are an abomination to his soul."

Things certainly have changed since 1922, when Emily Post wrote, "A man and a woman went out from Bar Harbor and did not return until the next day. Everyone knew the fog had come in as thick as pea soup, but to the end of time—her reputation will suffer from the experience."

Yes, indeed, things have changed. But Emily had one piece of advice that still works today: "When in doubt, consult the Ten Commandments of the Holy Bible." Right on, Emily.

For the Love of Plants

There has been a lot of controversy, pro and con, about the value of talking to plants. Not too many years ago, anyone who talked to plants was considered a little bit dotty—someone who didn't have both oars in the water. But then there was a brief period of time when it was considered very hip to talk to one's plants, and many people found new hope that their windowsills would soon resemble small jungles of rolling foliage—just by encouraging plants with a few kind, complimentary words.

Now that the fad has faded, there is again a tendency to snicker at anyone who has *named* his plants, who greets the plants in the morning, or has a conversation with flowerpots during the day (although we have a producer here who planted an evergreen tree from a twig, talked to it every morning and evening—while friends and relatives laughed—and now has a balsam that's big enough to trim with lights at Christmastime).

Well, let the detractors snicker. Next time tell the snickerer that houseplants are more than decorative. They help clean the air. Studies conducted by NASA found that the greater the number of indoor plants, the healthier it is for humans. Foliage plants, like the various ivies and flowers like daisies and mums remove—literally *remove*—poisonous benzene and carbon monoxide from the air. And they absorb large quantities of dangerous formaldehyde. Plants breathe in poison and exhale life-giving oxygen.

Why do they do that? God made them that way. Can they hear your thanks? Nobody knows absolutely whether plants are receptive to kind words and compliments. Does it make *you* feel better to talk to them? And urge them to live and grow? Then by all means, do it.

That First Break

I have a friend who is a writer. Now, that in itself is no big deal, because most of us have taken a crack at writing—although it isn't our main source of income.

This man writes for a *living*, and in a rather extended career has written several thousand—not hundreds, but thousands—of television and radio shows. He's won many awards including the Writer's Guild Award and the Peabody Award for his scripting.

I once asked him why he decided to become a writer. He said he didn't really have writing on his list of career choices, but when he was only a junior in high school, and going through a difficult period of his life, his high school teacher felt he had a pretty good way with words and took the time to really encourage him to put things down on paper. She suggested he work for the local paper during the summer and, in time, writing just became something he did. Whenever he had a particular success, he wrote to that teacher. He never forgot the role she played in his life.

Someone saw something in *you* once. That's partly why you're where you are today. It could have been a thoughtful parent, a perceptive teacher, a demanding drill sergeant, an appreciative employer —or just a friend who dug down in his pocket and came up with a few bucks. Whoever it was had the kindness and the foresight to bet on your future.

Those are two beautiful qualities that separate the human being from other animals.

Here's a suggestion: In the next day or so, take ten minutes to write a grateful note to the person who helped you. You'll keep a wonderful friendship alive. As a matter of fact, take an extra ten minutes and give somebody else a break.

Who knows? Someday you might get a nice letter. It could be one of the most gratifying messages you ever read.

Reading the Bible

*H*ow many of you read the Bible more than once a day? Surprisingly, fewer than 2 percent of you—according to a survey taken for a book called *One Hundred Percent American.*

Now there's no one keeping score on how many times you look at the Good Book each day—and the amount of Bible reading you do offers no direct guarantee that you'll get to heaven. What's important about Bible reading is that this is a Book that is filled with rich spiritual treasures.

If you are looking for adventure, you'll find more of it in the Bible than any other book you could possibly read. The Bible affords adventure in epic proportions. From the Great Flood to the passion of Christ—there are stories that are repeated, adapted, rewritten, retold, remade, and dramatized, because the stories themselves are so powerful—the messages and the morals are so strong that even in this contemporary world they are absolutely irresistible.

There is poetry in the Bible, too. Nothing is more moving than Matthew or Luke's recounting the story of the nativity. Some passages of the Bible have been set to music. Other passages have been borrowed for the titles of books and plays.

The Bible is probably the most utilitarian piece of literature ever created by humans. It's often said that every problem of man, every victory, every emotion, every word of hope, and the description of every sin is contained in this one Book. And that's about right.

When Woodrow Wilson was president, he read the Bible every day, and he's quoted as saying, "It is one of the most singular books in the world. Every time you open it, some old text you have read a score of times suddenly beams with new meaning."

I find that very true. It's really *some Book.*

Just Ask

When she was seventeen, she was the editor of her high school yearbook. The theme that year was "The Media." She thought it would be a great idea to get pictures and statements from some of the network anchor people, but she doubted that any of them would respond to a high school student from a small village.

In those days, Chet Huntley was the leading news figure in New York and she felt that if she could get his picture and a comment it would be sensational; but she didn't know how to go about reaching him. She imagined banks of secretaries, desk assistants, and publicity people blocking her way. She asked her father, "How could I talk with Chet Huntley?"

"Call NBC and ask to talk to him."

With great trepidation, she dialed the NBC number. The operator said, "One moment, please," and the next voice she heard was a man, who said, simply, "Huntley." She asked, and he agreed, provided she could come to his office in New York. "It never occurred to me to just ask," she recalled.

That little story fits a study made by the University of Alberta. One hundred sixty students were asked to evaluate fifteen different methods of getting someone to cooperate. The number one method was, simply, asking. "If you want somebody to do a favor for you, don't try to manipulate them into it. Just ask them."

Asking, they say, works better than anything. Buttering people up, bargaining with them, threatening or making an emotional appeal were all viewed negatively. When you simply ask, you're not looking for special favors or offering any favors. You are being direct.

I think the reason so many people hate to ask is that they fear rejection. There can be nothing more humiliating or mortifying to the human spirit than rejection of any kind. Many very devout people even feel very afraid to ask God for anything. And my question to them is—why?

There are many things we should take directly to the Lord in prayer. You can't manipulate Jesus Christ, but you can ask Him. And He wants you to. Think about it.

Worrywarts

*T*he world abounds with worrywarts. And a psychologist named Elinor Kinarthy of Rio Hondo College in California has worked out a test that should tell you whether you're a worrywart or not. You are a worrywart if:

- After having an important conversation with a fellow worker or a friend, you think you've said all the wrong things.
- When your mate or your child is late, you worry the *minute* they're late that the very worst has happened.
- When you have to make a decision—which car to buy or whether to take a job you've been offered—you either don't make the decision or you try to get somebody else to make it for you.
- A friend drops over unexpectedly and you feel terrible that your friend is seeing your house in its natural state.
- When you leave work at the end of the day, you think of something that may have gone wrong and you worry about it. You even lose sleep over it.

Or—try this one: You didn't get that promotion at work. You fear you're in danger of being fired. You stew and fret.

Or how about this? Your friend doesn't really want to talk to you and probably doesn't like you after all. And when people in a room are laughing, you assume they're laughing at you.

If you recognize yourself in even two or three of these situations, you are a worrywart. And you're not having a very good time. Why not go to the Good Book for help. Take for instance, the line in Exodus 14:13 that says, "Fear not! Stand your ground and you will see the victory the Lord will win for you today."

Or, as the song says, "Don't worry, Be happy." You'll live longer.

Where's the Middle in "Middle Age"?

A couple of parishioners were standing in the back of the church last Sunday talking about their kids. I had seen those kids when they were newlyweds and asked the parents how they were doing. They were doing well. The parents were now grand-parents, and suddenly one mother gasped, "Oh, my! Do you realize our children are pushing middle age?

There was a momentary deathly silence. I assured them that age is two things: a state of mind and a different set of worries. Chronologically, middle age is somewhere between the ages of 45 and 65. (To be generous.)

You are middle-aged if you don't recognize the name of music groups on the radio. You never heard of Guns N' Roses, M. C. Hammer, or Christopher Cross. You are middle-aged if you take a day or two to recover from strenuous exercise... and you worry about having enough money to take care of future medical problems.

You realize that when you were in your twenties and thirties you often wished that your children were grown-up and gone. You realize that all kids are noisy and spoiled, except, of course, your grand-children. You find yourself glancing at the obituary column now and then just to check out the ages. You find yourself actually beginning to worry about your retirement. You have decided for the fifteenth time to start dieting next week. You have quit smoking and have become rather nasty about people who light up within half a mile of you.

And further: You're coming to church services more often and with greater regularity. You remember when you were 18 and felt you were immortal. You want to assure yourself through your faith that there's nothing to worry about.

And if your faith is strong—there really isn't.

All You Really Need to Know

Week after week, month after month, and, yes, year after year, the *New York Times* reports that author Robert Fulghum sells more books than just about anybody else in the civilized world. He was the first author in the history of the *Times* to capture the number one and number two spots on the same best-seller list.

What was it about what he had to say in his books that caused so many people to buy them and then buy them again for their friends?

In his first book—*All I Really Need to Know I Learned in Kindergarten*—this Unitarian minister from Seattle writes simply, about simple things. His books are collections of essays he's written before, but they have now swept the nation.

What does he say? He says, "Share everything. Don't hit people. Put things back where you found them. Clean up your own mess. Don't take things that aren't yours. Say you're sorry when you hurt somebody. Wash your hands before you eat. Flush the toilet. Take a nap every afternoon. When you go out in the world, watch out for traffic. Hold hands and stick together. Be aware of wonder. Be aware of the Dick and Jane books—and the first word you ever learned. The biggest word of all— "look!"

What Robert Fulghum has done is what your priest, minister, or rabbi tries to do: remind you that your own good sense is all you really need to get by in this world. You *are* capable of kindness, forgiveness, patience and understanding, and you *are* smart enough to take care of yourself.

But it's human nature to want to complicate things. Make life harder than it has to be. Just consider two things: What if *everybody* put things back where they belonged and cleaned up their own mess; wouldn't it be a great world?

Getting Along

*I*t will take a long time for Americans to forget the Los Angeles riots—and not just because they involved the president or the National Guard or looting or senseless violence, but because they stirred the national conscience and made us all wonder whether it would ever be possible for all of us to get along.

Many surveys were taken (surveys are always taken when problems make news), but *USA Today* printed a few remarks that I liked. These are thoughts from middle America. Nearly everyone who was asked said, "Yes, we can get along, but . . . ."

A man in Winter Park, Florida, said, "We not only can get along in this country, but it's mandatory that we do. All Americans should work very diligently to ensure that all citizens are treated fairly and equally, not only in the court system, in the workplace, and in the marketplace, but in all aspects of society."

Then there was this: "As individuals, we have to look to God and the teachings of our religions to be guided in our everyday actions. The hearts of people have to be changed to be more accepting, less prejudicial. All people have to accept responsibility for their own actions and their own behavior."

And here's another: "We have to just quit being so selfish and quit thinking of ourselves. It's getting to be too much of a 'me' society. It happens when little groups pull for what they think is right for them, and they don't look at the big picture."

Well, that's a cross section. But the real problem is this: How do we tame the greedy? How do we teach the hotheaded, the uneducated, the uninformed, the bullies, the bloodthirsty? There aren't enough teachers—there aren't even enough jails. But we have to do it. As the man said, "it's mandatory."

Consider what the men who founded this nation look for when the situation was desperate and mandatory. They looked for spiritual strength. And they found it. A good place to start.

If It Doesn't Feel Right . . .

Would you take candy from a baby? That's a rather obtuse question. Of course you wouldn't. Would you refuse to help a blind person cross the street? Of course not. Now, these examples are extreme, but they show us the thought process that helps humans decide what's right and what's wrong.

I'm sure nobody ever showed you a list of what things are good and what things are bad. The list would be too long. God has given us instinctive tendencies that have helped us build a social structure in which we can live in comparative peace. We instinctively know the difference between right and wrong. It's a feeling we have.

There is also a mechanism built into us that gives us great joy when we see we have helped someone else. Some misconstrue this joy as being self-congratulatory—but it's the *giving* that triggers the feeling. Doing good things, being kind and considerate, and helping others is inbedded so strongly in many people that they couldn't imagine being any other way.

We all know a few saints. But many people are guilty of doing thoughtless things and they *know* it, because it *just doesn't feel right.* It's much like making a wrong turn in your car and knowing somehow that you haven't done the right thing. You are getting lost.

Most of the laws by which we live were fashioned to promote tranquility. Not all of them, of course, but that's what laws are really all about. If we didn't know the basics of right or wrong, we wouldn't need the confessional.

So the silent axiom that will make our lives much easier is—if it doesn't *feel* right, don't.

Fame and Fortune

*I*f you will pardon my directness, one of the most ridiculous scenes ever filmed was in the movie *42nd Street*, when Warner Baxter says to Ruby Keeler, "You're going out there a scared kid, but you're going to come back a star." She had learned the entire leading role of a big musical—songs and all— in just a few hours.

This one scene helped set a whole new set of fantasies for young people who want fame and fortune. It looks so great in the papers and it seems so glamorous on those television shows that appeal to the wannabes of this show-struck age. The very thought that one's image would be immortalized on film, on tape, in books, in the press—that you could leave a legacy of popularity long after you're gone. That while you are building that legacy, you will live a rhapsody of fun and deep content as people admire you and love you and wait on you.

Then, as time goes by, there is the wistful wondering—as the wannabe becomes the couldabeen. The sad part is that this desire is born within us to some degree, but it's nurtured by the media to the extent that it can actually be emotionally harmful to some people.

Consider fame for a moment . . . and its longevity. Who was Miss America two years ago? Can you name five movie stars from thirty years ago? Where was the last Miss Universe Pageant held? How long does a hit song stay on the charts? (A week? A month? A year?) Not very long as we measure time.

There is nothing wrong with fantasizing *or* daydreaming. What's important is this: While you are waiting to be discovered, work hard at being the best human being you can be. Be the best "you"— and you'll be surprised how popular you'll become.

Worldly Wisdom

*T*hree hundred years ago, a Jesuit scholar in Spain had become a keen observer of the ways of the world, and he put together a number of mini-messages on ethical behavior.

Today, three centuries later, Baltasar Gracian has become a literary lion. In a book called *The Art of Worldly Wisdom* he offers advice such as this:

> Don't talk about yourself. You must either praise yourself, which is vanity, or criticize yourself, which is meekness. You show a lack of good judgment and are a nuisance to others. Nor is it prudent to talk about people who are present. You risk running aground on flattery.

Another bit of Gracian's advice that I rather like is:

> Be known for your courtesy—it alone can make you worthy of praise. Courtesy is the best part of culture, a kind of enchantment, and it wins the goodwill of all, just as rudeness wins only scorn and universal annoyance. When rudeness comes from pride, it is detestable; when from bad breeding it is contemptible. Better too much courtesy than too little. Treat your enemies with courtesy, and you'll see how valuable it really is. It costs little but pays a nice dividend.

One modern critic called Gracian "a Machiavelli with scruples." It's a little late for criticism of any kind, but what makes this small volume interesting is that the preachments and admonitions of three hundred years ago are appropriate today.

A little bit like an expanded Book of Proverbs. Proverbs is probably a little more poetic. For example, this advice (9:12): "If you are wise, it is to your own advantage; and, if you are arrogant, you alone shall bear it."

Rules of the Game of Life

More sage advice from the pen of Baltasar Gracian, this time from his list of three hundred rules of life, called "The Aphorisms."

These were strong suggestions, and I think merit our attention. In the interest of space, I share but a handful—all excellent food for thought:

- Reach perfection.
- Don't outshine your boss. (I don't know if those two are compatible anymore.)
- Associate with those you can learn from.
- Don't have a single imperfection. (Wouldn't that be something? How would we know?)
- Weigh matters carefully.
- Be well-informed.
- Adapt to those around you.

Some of his preachments have become bromides. For example:

- Quit while you're ahead. (How many times have you heard *that*?)
- Avoid grief. (Easier said than done.)
- It's better to be intensive than extensive.
- Be righteous and firm.
- Know your best quality.
- Take care to make things turn out well.
- Use grace in dealing with others.

- Know how to wait. (The most painful lesson an American can learn.)
- Don't give in to every common impulse.

While all three hundred of Baltasar's tips have some merit (he was very hip for his day), somehow I keep returning to the Ten Commandments.

The "shalt nots" are not very aesthetic, but they still make all the points that have to be made.

. . . When You Grow Up?

"Sooo. What do you want to be when you grow up?" What youngster hasn't endured that inquisition too many times? As if the adult really cared, instead of just trying to make childish conversation.

Well, much to my delight, the Sesame Place Kids Poll asked 450 youngsters that very question and got some rather surprising answers. . . answers you wouldn't expect from a preteener, let alone a preschooler. In fact, the very youngest accounted for the biggest response, and 38 percent of *them* said they wanted to be—happily married. *Happily married*. And that 38 percent was the largest single response.

Does that say something about family life? Were their parents unhappy? Or were they being raised by parents who often demonstrated their love for each other? If you think your children don't know what's going on in your home, you may be amazed.

Of the younsters who were polled, 24 percent said they wanted to be rich. Nineteen percent said they wanted to be healthy, and 14 percent said they wanted to be famous—or popular—or surrounded by their friends.

I recall vividly being asked that question any number of times, and I also remember coming up with an answer I was quite sure the adult wanted to hear—cowboy, fireman, police officer. And so the survey amused me and made me think that children are becoming a lot more sophisticated.

Not one child answered the survey by saying he or she wanted to be an astronaut, a nurse, a doctor or a fireperson. Forget cowboy and cowgirl altogether. And did any little boy or girl aspire to be the president of the United States? Not one. Young people are very aware these days.

You just can't kid kids.

The Real Mother Goose

"*L*ittle Jack Horner sat in a corner eating his Christmas pie. He put in his thumb and pulled out a plum and said, 'What a good boy am I!'"

A simple nursery rhyme from old Mother Goose. Everybody knows it and can recite it—but what does it mean? "Little Jack Horner" is about a political scandal. In the sixteenth century there were no scandal sheets or radio gossips, and certainly no trash TV shows...so the way word got around was in little rhymes and jingles that people sang in local taverns and behind safe doors at home.

The Annotated Mother Goose tells us that Thomas Horner, the last of the abbots of Glastonbury Cathedral in England—during the time of the Dissolution of the Church—decided he would try to get on the good side of King Henry VIII. You see, Henry was not only accumulating wives, he was taking over all the church property he could get his hands on. So the abbot sent his steward, a fellow named Jack, to London with a Christmas gift for the king. It was a pie—with a heavy top crust. In the pie were hidden the deeds to twelve manorial estates.

On the way to London, Jack opened the pie slightly and extracted one deed—the manor of Mells. Quite a plum, indeed. This thievery was joked about by the citizens until King Henry heard about it. What happened? Well, Henry got the deed back, and little Jack got hanged—beheaded and quartered. So the merry jingle of the London pub was really a story of plunder, thievery, violence, and death.

There are many happy little verses that children still recite that have mind-boggling stories behind them. The only words that seemed to have survived the Dissolution pretty much intact were the ones not even Henry VIII could banish. The words of the Holy Bible.

More Mother Goose

We just looked at Mother Goose rhymes, and how they grew out of social scandals in the sixteenth century. No one had a Bill of Rights in those days and certainly there was no First Amendment. So people had to watch what they said.

Now, take "Jack and Jill," a perfectly harmless little ditty: "Jack and Jill went up the hill to fetch a pail of water. Jack fell down and broke his crown—and Jill came tumbling after." Lower-class Britons would follow this rhyme with a great laugh.

One explanation was that King Henry VIII—just before he threw off the supremacy of the Pope—thought it would be a great idea to send a trusted advisor and a crowned theologian to Rome to get the Pope to bless his divorce and remarriage to a younger woman. They would bring back a container of holy water to prove the Pope's agreement. Jack was the crowned theologian and Jill was not a girl, but a man whose name was spelled G.I.L.L.E. Rome was the hill. The two men went up to Rome and, according to *The Annotated Mother Goose*, laid the request on the Pope. And the Pope in that day did about what the Pope in this day would do: He told them there was no way. King or no king, a life of serial wives was out.

So the rhyme says, in effect, that Jack and Jill were kicked off the hill and didn't even get any holy water to bring back to Henry. Henry was not pleased. Jack fell from grace and lost his crown, and Jill came tumbling after.

You didn't know that, as a child, you were reciting ancient European religious history, did you?

Prayer

*T*he noted evangelist Billy Graham tells this story on himself. During his city-to-city crusades, he made it a practice to pray for specific people in each city. He often would write the mayor or various members of the upper political echelon and ask them for a list of people they felt he should pray for.

Before going to one city, he wrote his usual letter to the mayor asking for a list of those in need of special prayers. The mayor responded by sending him a copy of the city directory.

What the mayor implied, I think, is certainly true. We are all in need of prayer. One of the problems of being human is that we can think, and feel guilt, and feel self-conscious about our shortcomings—and we really have nobody with whom to discuss all we feel. Here's where prayer comes in.

When we pray, what happens? Usually our mood changes. Our thoughts focus on God. We are able to be sincere and honest about the things that worry us most, whatever they are. In prayer we are showing concern for ourselves, and that's the first step in solving any problem we might have. And we're taking our case to the Lord in prayer.

Now, let's talk about praying for somebody *else*. If you can bring yourself to pray for a friend—or even for someone you might consider an enemy— here's what happens. You'll find that it's practically impossible to pray for someone and hate them at the same time. If resentment and ill will are rising up in you, take it to the Lord in prayer. And don't stop praying. No prayer is ever wasted.

And while you pray for others, remember this: You cannot kneel in prayer without benefit to yourself. When you tell God, you also tell yourself—and I can't think of any better therapy.

Whatever joins us to God is good.

Where Is God?

The Bible is full of parables, and they do a pretty good job of making moral points. The story form is so delightful that in more modern times, writers and philosophers have come up with a few of their own which are told and retold, slightly revised as they pass from teller to teller, but the point is always made. One of my favorites is called "Where Is God?"

There was once a woman who was very religious and devout and filled with the love of God. Each morning she would walk many blocks to go to church. Sick or well she made a daily pilgrimage to that church, entered silently, and knelt to pray. She was in God's house. And every day on her way to church, children called to her, beggars would accost her, but she was so immersed in her devotions that she didn't even see them. Now, one day she walked down the street in her customary manner and arrived at the church just in time for services. She pushed on the door but it would not open. She pushed again—harder—and found the door was locked. Distressed at the thought that she would miss the service for the first time in many years, she looked up. And there, right before her face, she found a note pinned to the door. It said, "I'M OUT HERE!"

That's a parable that should hit home. It's nice to be devout. Every parish needs its loyal church-goers. But God is elsewhere, too. When you look into the eyes of a distressed mother who could use your help and comfort, a friend who has lost his way, an aged neighbor who can't get to church alone—God is looking with you.

Actually, Godliness begins the moment you leave God's house.

Parables and Television

A pastor I know was asked by an anxious mother, "If the Bible uses parables to teach, doesn't television do the same—only with more impact? And don't television shows send the wrong messages with a tremendous force on our young people?" Well, the answers to those questions are yes and yes.

Once upon a time, the networks and stations were very careful about the gratuitous use of violence and sex in television productions. We have a network writer on our staff who remembers vividly the days of twin beds for married couples and the three-second kiss. Those were the days of live TV—and shows like "Mama," "The Life of Riley," and "The Ed Sullivan Show."

Then Hollywood took over and convinced television that it wasn't showing "real life." That real life is decapitation, bloody gun battles, exploding cars, police chases, foul language, and constant concentration on sex. So sex, violence and dirty words became more and more frequent in movies, hence the home screen.

Hollywood looks at our growing crime rate and assumes a "Gee whiz" attitude. While the movie moguls recline at their pools many miles from the Los Angeles riots, the news program on their big-screen television sets suggests that maybe they should have second thoughts about turning out movies in which the body count numbers twenty or more. But those second thoughts are quickly dismissed when *their* Bible—*Variety*—reports that *Lethal Weapon 3* grossed over $70 million in only eleven days. The moviemaker shrugs and says, "What do you want from me? This is a business. This is what the people want and I give it to them."

And the parables are told, and the crime rate soars.

Nuking the Moon

As if we didn't have enough to worry about what with global warming and the high crime rate, now a few scientists say they've figured out a way to blow up the moon. These men of physics ask what good is it anyway? The moon causes a rash of idle romantic promises. It causes a lot of strange people to act even stranger, and it plays with our oceans.

A mathematics professor from Iowa State University says if we nuked the moon and fixed it so that part or all of it would fall into the Pacific Ocean, the earth would become a Garden of Eden. A place where no one would go hungry.

Dr. Alexander Abian says if the moon fell into the ocean, it would push our planet into a more favorable alignment with the sun and improve the ecology. We'd have a more even distribution of sun rays and we wouldn't have those brutal winters and scorching summers. It would be springtime all year round.

The earth now has a sixty-six-degree tilt relative to the plane of its orbit. It's the tilt that causes the seasons. And just removing the moon would correct the tilt. It would be the moon plowing into the Pacific Ocean that would jolt the earth just enough to straighten it up.

Well, I worry about that. With my limited knowledge of the profound sciences, I concluded it would be a bad idea. First, it assaults my theology. God put the moon there and put us here, and it's a project that is really beyond mere mortals. Second, the jolt would have the impact of a thousand earth-quakes—and that would be hard on the nerves.

I suggest we leave things the way God created them. He is, after all, the master builder. We are but the abusers of His works.

Competing with God

A guide was conducting a tour through one of the nation's famous chemical works that turned out a very popular synthetic thread. He led the visitors through the twenty-two separate operations it took to manufacture the thread, and told the tourists that while the whole operation took four days, he thought his company had actually improved on God.

Hardly.

Consider the common spider. A spider makes its thread in *one* operation instead of twenty-two. It doesn't require several days, either. The spider's operation takes only a split second. By the time the thread *extrudes* from the spider's *spinnerets* and reaches the hind legs, it is cured and sustains its total weight.

Furthermore, one single thread of a spider is composed of one-thousand individual filaments. That's why the spider's thread dries instantly. In addition to all that, the spider carries its factory, plus raw materials, in its own body. No manufacturer anywhere—no creator of goods—can match God's own mineaturization.

God is the greatest craftsman of all. All you need do for confirmation is to step outdoors. Look about you. Who created the complex life forms in those little flowers along your sidewalk? Why are those blooms facing the sun? Who told them to? Sure, *you* put them there, but who makes them work?

Everywhere you look, you see God's work. That plane flying over your house. Certainly the work of man, but where did the man get the *idea*? From God's creatures—the *birds*. And all the material—all the mass that is reshaped for human use—originally came from God.

There is absolutely no competing with God. We can learn from God—but we can't *begin* to compete with God.

The Swahili Proverbs

As accents change from one part of the country to another—and as languages change from one part of the world to another—we're inclined to laugh and find amusement in the proverbs of another country. It all depends on your point of view.

I came across a few proverbs from East Africa which Father Miles Riley, a traveling missionary, found, and, at first blush, they sound strange, but look carefully at these Swahili proverbs. They should become ours, too:

- When the elephants fight, the grass gets hurt.
- I pointed out to you the moon, but all you saw was my finger.
- Patience is the key to tranquility.
- The water in a coconut shell is like an ocean to an ant.
- A visitor is a guest for two days; on the third day give the person a hoe.
- A slow rain bears the most fruit.

There are also the little short adages that are repeated often, such as, "Hurry, hurry has no blessing," and, "Education is an ocean." And this one would be indiginous to East African women *or* men: "To marry off your son is to swallow a stone."

So while the proverbs assume the point of view of the land from which they come—there is wisdom here.

Every society has its proverbs. its philosophies, its manners, its ideologies—and almost all of them are akin to the proverbs we find in our own Bible. Proverbs are axioms that are meant to serve as easy-to-remember pieces of automatic wisdom. Every proverb recites its own homily.

Sometime, pick up the Good Book—turn to Proverbs and refresh your memory. Couldn't hurt.

What Do We Need?

It seems that we Americans have a compulsion—not a desire, but a compulsion—toward the acquiring of "things." Material things.

I must say that having things can give one pleasure. There are technical things that offer speed and convenience. But we also have a habit of coveting the things our neighbors have—the things that Madison Avenue tells us are hip and smart and "in." We compare our things to the things others have—and we tend to feel a little superior when we come across someone who has less, and extremely inferior when we come across someone who has more.

Often we pay a great price for our desires when we put them ahead of our real needs. Going into deep debt to acquire something that will feed our psyche fills us with a feeling of regret almost from the moment we acquire it. And we must ask ourselves—especially in these very shaky economic times—do we really *need* it? Not just do we need it, but do we *really* need it.

We hear of celebrities buying more glamorous clothes than they can ever wear, of rich sports figures owning more cars than they can ever drive. For the most part they live lives of fearful pretension—of pathological apprehension. It reminds me of an old parable:

Once upon a time, an Indian monk in his travels found a precious stone and kept it. One day he met a traveler, and when he opened his bag to share his provisions with him, the traveler saw the jewel and asked the monk to give it to him. The monk did so, much to the amazement of the traveler. The traveler departed, overjoyed with the unexpected gift of the precious stone. Now he would have wealth and security for the rest of his life.

However, a few days later, he came back and found the monk, and gave him back the stone. The traveler said, "Now give me something more precious than this stone, valuable as it is. Give me that which enabled you to give it to me."

God in "America"

It's a little difficult to explain why God is in the Congress every day and mentioned copiously in the great songs about our land and yet is banned from public schools and parks.

In 1893, Katherine Lee Bates ascended Pikes Peak in Colorado and was inspired by what she called the "spacious skies"—and as she looked down, other words went through her mind—"Purple mountain majesties," and "amber waves of grain." This, of course, was the genesis of her great hymn, "America the Beautiful." And the first stanza ends with, "America! America! God shed His grace on thee. And crown thy good with brotherhood from sea to shining sea."

Many people say they prefer this hymn to "The Star-Spangled Banner," which is really a story of war. The argument will rage on. But Katherine Bates' hymn closes each verse with a deep yearning prayer for God to grant the higher gifts to America—to mend its flaws, refine its gold, and "confirm thy soul in self-control, thy liberty in law."

What a poignant prayer! It is, indeed, a prayer, and I'm sure every child has sung it at least once—in school. I don't mean to get political here, but I see no harm in praising those pilgrims in Ms. Bates' song who beat a thoroughfare for freedom across the wilderness.

Katherine Bates says this about her hymn:

We must match the greatness of our country with the goodness of personal Godly living. Greatness and goodness are not necessarily synonymous. Rome was great, but she was not good, and the Roman Empire fell. Unless we're willing to crown our greatness with goodness, our beloved America could go the same way.

Then there are the very famous words of Irving Berlin. "God—yes—God Bless America!"

Panic and Prayer

*H*undreds of thousands of suburbanites who trek into New York City every day probably suffer as much stress as anyone in the world—and that's only what they go through *getting* to work and *coming* home.

Many commuters actually suffer severe panic when the trains are too crowded, the subways too hot, the buses too late and the traffic in gridlock. Sweat beads on the brow. Your knees turn to jelly. Your heart races. Your stomach churns. Fatigue batters every bone. You feel you're going to pass out, but you're afraid of looking foolish or causing a commotion. So you hang on, telling yourself that if you ever get home, you'll never step outside the house again.

But, somehow you make it through. So by 6:30 the next morning you're willing to try it one more time.

Of course, panic doesn't belong exclusively to the commuter set. It happens to a lot of people. Maybe *most* people—at least once in a while. Psychiatrists will tell you to find a place where you can relax for a moment. Take a deep breath. Better yet, take several deep breaths.

And I would suggest adding a little word of prayer. Remind yourself that when you have the Lord you're not alone. You'll be surprised at how much sharing your distress with Him can help *you*.

Dr. Michael H. Grant, a relaxation expert at Lenox Hill Hospital, says, "If you are prone to such attacks, try visiting a church or a temple for a half hour or so every once in a while. You need a place where you can turn off the mania and let your anxieties rest for a little while." And you'll find how soothing and refreshing a short prayer can be.

In any situation that tends to be traumatic, it helps to have somebody to talk it out with. And who better than He who knows exactly what you're talking about?

Signed, Anonymous

*T*he most prolific author in the world—creator of more words than Shakespeare, Bacon, and Saint Luke combined—is a person called "Anonymous." "Anon" for short. His or her writings cross my desk daily, and a few are quite good, I think. Like this list of rules guaranteed to make life easier:

- If you open it, close it.
- If you turn it on, turn it off.
- If you unlock it, lock it up.
- If you break it, admit it.
- If you can't fix it, get someone who can.
- If you borrow it, return it.
- If you value it, take care of it.
- If you make a mess, clean it up.
- If you move it, put it back.
- If it belongs to someone else and you want to use it, get permission.
- If you don't know how to work it, leave it alone.
- If it's none of your business, don't ask questions.
- If it ain't broke, don't fix it. *And—*
- If it will brighten someone's day, say it!

I love the last one. If we could remember *only that.* How difficult would it be to notice one nice thing about somebody else—and mention it? You don't have to make a big production out of it. And if you can accomplish that *one little thing* on a day that you, yourself, are feeling lousy and at odds with the world, you'll be surprised to see what it does to your own disposition.

You could even have a nice day.

Withholding Judgment

*T*hings are not always what they seem. And that goes for people, too.

Back in the days when an ice cream sundae cost a lot less than it does now, a little boy—about 10 years old—walked into a hotel coffee shop and sat at a table. A waitress put a glass of water in front of him. The little boy asked: "How much is an ice cream sundae?" "Fifty cents," the waitress said. The little boy pulled his hand out of his pocket and looked at the number of coins in it. "How much is a plain dish of ice cream?" he asked.

Some people were now waiting for a table, and the waitress was becoming a little impatient. "Thirty-five cents," she said brusquely.

This time the little boy counted his coins. The waitress sighed. "I'll have the plain ice cream," he said. Well, the waitress brought the ice cream, put the bill on the table and walked away. The boy finished the ice cream, paid the cashier and walked out the door.

When the waitress came back, she picked up the boy's empty plate and then swallowed hard at what she saw. There—placed neatly beside the empty dish—were two nickels and five pennies. Her tip. If the boy hadn't considered a tip, he could have had the chocolate sundae.

Now, fifteen cents wasn't going to change the lifestyle of that waitress, but she did learn something.

Even little people can be considerate. The people you least expect to share will surprise you.

God doesn't pass out pins that say "I'm considerate, so love me." It's only a guess at best—and anyone who says, "I can tell what a person's like when I first see him," is being neither correct nor considerate.

Doing Dumb Things

*H*ave you ever done or said something really dumb —something that really affected your life or even your feeling of well-being? Something you would take back if you had the chance? Most of us probably have.

But we can learn something from a serious gaffe. If we reenact the event in our minds, we'll most likely find that we acted in a fit of hostility. And the hostility may not have been directed at the person who actually bothered us. We might have been mad at ourselves...or a hundred other things.

Scientific data suggest that we make our biggest mistakes when we're in a hostile mood. Of course, we live in a very competitive world where nice guys finish last. But this we know for sure: Hostility interferes with our creative thinking. We do dumb things when we're very upset.

And we know something else. Hostiliity isn't good for our heart. In fact, with the exception of deep grief, hostility is the worst emotion your heart can endure. You can literally kill yourself with hate.

It's tough not to be cynical in this day and age— but when you begin to mistrust others to the extent that you bring on hate, try this: Confess your hostility and seek support for a change. Reason with yourself. Ask yourself, *Why am I so upset? Why am I letting this eat me alive?* Then try—at least try— trusting other people.

Force yourself to listen more. Substitute assertiveness for aggression. Laugh at yourself and practice relaxing. Finally, pretend today is your last day on earth—and practice forgiveness.

And if you still need help, ask your priest, minister, or rabbi.

How Old Is Old?

Many psychologists and medical professionals agree that the more active we are in our later years, the better we'll feel and the longer we'll live.

Age is certainly a factor, but consider this. A hockey player is in the twilight of his career at age 30. A professional football player is an old man at age 35. So athletes, in particular, have to begin completely new lives as they approach middle age. They know they must adjust—they know the body can't take the kind of punishment it was once subjected to.

It's likewise with people over 50, 60, or 70. George Bernard Shaw won the Nobel Prize when he was 69. Golda Meir was 71 when she became prime minister of Israel. Jessica Tandy was 80 when she won her first Academy Award for *Driving Miss Daisy.* Benjamin Franklin was one of the authors of the Constitution when he was 81. George Burns is booked into the Palladium in London on his 100th birthday.

The fact of the matter is that age is as much a state of mind as it is a state of physical being. It's a fact today that people are living longer. And the worst thing your body can experience is a sudden drop in activity. The same goes for the mind. If you've been active for three score and ten years, you can't just give up.

And you can't feel that nobody needs you. A lot of people need you. Call your pastor. Ask him about volunteer work. You'll be surprised to realize the joy and satisfaction you can get by doing something for the Lord.

Rotten Times

I guess we've all had those days when absolutely nothing goes right. And who hasn't put down the newspaper in tacit despair after reading about what human beings are doing to each other.

Well, now there's a monthly newsletter for the disenchanted and the unemployed—called *Rotten Times*. Just hearing that title makes one feel that maybe its timing is rotten, too. At first I didn't know whether to laugh or be disturbed that making fun of hardship is not funny.

But there is a rather sound philosophy about *Rotten Times*, believe it or not. According to Hal Giesking, the publisher, economists are citing statistics and percentages and numbers to show there's a recovery. "But you can't eat statistics," he says. "Two million jobs have been lost in this recession, and if yours was one," Giesking says, "all you know is that you're forty-two, have kids in school, and have a mortgage to pay."

He explains that *Rotten Times* tries to make the nation's 9 million unemployed look on the bright side. "It's about hope," he says. "It's about success and economic survival in the nineties."

Hal Giesking is a former advertising executive who decided to become a writer. His first edition had a circulation of two hundred. It featured job tips, warnings about phony job ads, and stories of successful new businesses. His big worry about the success of *Rotten Times* is that it costs $12.95 to subscribe. That could be a deterrent. But I like the accent on hope.

It echoes what we read in Psalms 9:18. "For the needy shall not always be forgotten, nor shall the hope of the afflicted forever perish." Have hope.

Risk Taking

We could learn a serious lesson from the way children play.

A little girl I know takes a wooden mixing spoon, ties a string to it, and pretends it's a microphone and she's a famous rock singer. She even imitates the roar of the crowd. A little boy gets on a computer and pretends he's a famous writer—and he knocks out very fanciful stories. Still another youngster puts a handle on a wooden box and pretends it's a guitar and *he's* all five members of Guns N' Roses.

Well, we tend to smile at children's fantasies. Yet we have our own fantasies, too. More than one person I know sings in the bathtub. More than one person I know does the Walter Mitty thing. Yet, when it comes to fulfilling those fantasies, we seem to become very shy and practical. We want to write a book but we think we can't. We'd *like* to sing but we're sure we can't carry a tune. We know we'd be in heaven if we could play the piano or paint a picture.

Danny DeVito wanted to be an actor, and it never occurred to him that no one would cast a short, stout, balding man in a leading role.

Oprah Winfrey used to look in the mirror and imagine herself in front of a camera—even though she was a product of a broken home and was threatened with reform school.

The world is filled with dreamers. But too few dreamers are willing to become risk takers. Don't be afraid to let a little fantasy into your life. Don't listen to those who say, "You can't do it that way." Don't listen to that little voice of fear inside you. Don't be afraid to take a chance you want to take, to try to make a dream come true.

If Michelangelo had listened to those who said he couldn't do it—he would have painted the Sistine *floor*, and it would surely have been rubbed out by now.

The Stars and Us

When we look into the sky on a clear night we are absolutely awed by the number of stars we see. It boggles the brain.

Galileo claimed to have seen more than five thousand stars through his simple telescope. When I was in the seminary they were already talking about 250 million. Today scientists are tossing around words like *metagalaxies* and *ultra galaxies*—and even galaxies that have galaxies.

The universe is too big to see, let alone comprehend. The biggest telescope can only see a little part of it. Where does it begin and where does it end? And where did it all come from? When we contemplate these questions, it's difficult to understand how God can and does care for us as individuals. Considering the teeming billions—not millions—billions of people on our own planet we may find it hard to believe that God loves us all—as individuals.

Jesus taught us a great truth—that God is a father, and He will not forget even one of His children. The stories of the Bible tell us how Christ spent His time on earth, with all kinds of individuals— with holy people to be sure, but also with a beggar by a pool, with a woman of dubious reputation, with a troubled religous leader who asked for His help.

We know the story of the single lost sheep being of deep concern to the shepherd, of one coin being sought in the dust, of a missing son being welcomed back home. The stories are symbolic. They have been told to help us understand.

Of *course* the universe is vast and complex. But look into the miracle that is each of *us*. How could anything be more complex than the human body? And where did we begin? Who dreamed us up? The same great force that put all those stars in the sky.

Important to God? Of course we are. Every one of us.

The Garden of the Mind

"*A*s a person thinks in his heart, so he is." It's an old aphorism, but profound and true. The thoughts we create in our minds make us what we are and what we will become. We are literally what we think.

God gave us the ability to think, reason, plan, react and create. Our brains weren't made by machines. God allows us to be the master of our thoughts and energies. And within this complicated process there is the ability to discover, to analyze, to experience.

We have the ability to acquire wisdom. We have the ability to create power. This gift of God's is almost too much to contemplate. There is practically nothing that can't be conceived by the human mind. Imagine the force that God has unleashed within our human selves! And it can, in its extreme, be a force for great good or a force for great evil.

You might think of the mind as a garden. One garden might be neglected and its growth turned to weeds running wild—uncultivated and unkempt. Another garden is carefully cultivated, with clean rows of flowers and fruits. Both have gardeners, and the gardener is *you*.

Every person is what he is by how he makes his mind work. Just as a garden needs help to grow, so does the mind. Your mind is so powerful that it can help keep you well or make you desperately ill—even kill you. What's *in* your mind can be the seed of growth and happiness or the weeds of despair.

Grudges are weeds. Greed is certainly a weed. Weeds of the mind carry not only all the deadly sins but the greatest graces of God as well. So isn't it axiomatic that you can be either an evil spirit or an individual who is Godly and good? You only have to make up your mind. It's that simple. But first you must sow the seeds.

Where does one do this? May I suggest your nearest place of worship.

Children and
the Common Good

As the political rhetoric swirls about us at any time of any year, we hear grandiose verbiage about preparing ourselves for the twenty-first century, about cutting government spending so that the grandchildren of today won't be burdened with a tremendous debt.

Nice thought. But what we don't hear are facts like these:

- Every eight seconds of the school day, an American child drops out.
- Every thirteen seconds, an American child is abused or neglected.
- About every minute, a teenager has a baby.
- Every seven minutes, an American child is arrested for a drug offense.
- Every thirty minutes, an American child—that's right, child—is arrested for drunken driving.
- And every fifty-three minutes in our rich land, an American child dies because of poverty.

It's terrific, I think, for our many governments, local, state, and federal, to be so concerned about the state of our children two generations from now. It's the philosophical thing to do. But it seems to me we should be looking around at what's happening to our children today. It's more than just ironic that American children are poor at two to fourteen

times the rate of children in other developed coun-
tries. Nowhere is the paralysis of the public conscience more obvious than in how our people in
all our bureaus perceive our children. As a church,
we try our best. We track down and, yes, beg for
resources. But there has to be a whole new concern.

Next time you shake hands with a politician ask
him or her point blank, "What are you doing for
our children?" You may startle him—but he'll know
what's on your mind.

Remembering R. L. Stevenson

I was reciting a little verse to my niece the other day—a verse that was very popular when I was her age. It is by Robert Louis Stevenson, a British poet of long ago, who tried to explain the change of seasons. It goes:

In winter I get up at night
And dress by yellow candle light.
In summer, quite the other way,
I have to go to bed by day.

She had never heard it before, and I wondered how ol' Robert Louis Stevenson was faring with the rest of today's children who are smothered with "My Little Pony," "The Jetsons," talking Barbie dolls and kiddie rock.

If Stevenson is losing acceptance, it's too bad, because although he was known as a writer for children, he was, above all, a great philosopher with the ability to form great thoughts with simple words. He once wrote, for example:

That person is a success who has lived well, laughed often and loved much; who has gained the respect of intelligent people, and the love of children. That person is a success who has filled a unique niche and accomplished his or her task, who leaves the world better than before whether by a perfect poem or a rescued soul. It is a person who never lacked appreciation for the earth's beauty or failed to express it...who looked for the best in others and gave the best he or she had.

I have no idea whether Robert Louis Stevenson was a religious man, but if his writings reflect his soul—even his little nursery rhymes—then all religions could use many more people of his outlook.

How many will leave this earth with all those things accomplished? I have a notion Robert Louis Stevenson did.

New Kid on the Block

$H$is folks moved a lot, so he was always the new kid on the block. He was almost always on the defensive, always having to punch his way out of some encounter. He got used to hanging out alone. He was a depression kid, so he had to work, and it was through work that he discovered that the trials of life are also the opportunities.

His father was constantly out of work. Many times he and his dad would go from door to door looking for any kind of work at all—chopping wood, painting, fixing things. All the time he was developing a sense of self-reliance and imagination.

But amid all the struggle this big, ungainly kid was taught to play the piano by his mother. He got good enough to play for meals at a club in Oakland, California. He needed courage to keep going, but the piano won him some new friends and in time he drifted into acting.

First the stage and then in some of those movies that Hollywood calls "oaters." (Men chasing men on horses.)

It didn't seem like much at the time, but his father saw a future for this tall, grown-up boy who rode so high in the saddle. He says his father would have given him a college education if he could have —but there was just no money. Maybe it was a blessing.

There was something about this rugged guy that Hollywood directors started to notice and his parts began to get bigger. By then, television had come along, and there was a new market opening up for actors. Then his father died suddenly, but not before seeing his son in an episode from the series "Rawhide." His father was so proud, and told him "Now you've got to move—keep progressing or you'll decay." The status quo, his father said, was not good enough.

And so it was the hard times—and the courage— that made a star out of Clint Eastwood.

Jumping at Conclusions

One of our producers at Telicare said he had to lose ten pounds but the only exercise he was getting was jumping to conclusions. And jumping at them.

There's the ancient story of the master of a mansion who believed that his personal manservant was not working up to speed one day. At first he was merely annoyed when the servant was slow in laying the master's clothes. And he noticed that the servant was unusually quiet and introspective. Finally, the master blew his top and berated the servant at great length in front of the entire household. "Is there any excuse for such laziness?" he asked. A tear welled up in the servant's eyes and he said, "I'm not myself today. You see, my wife died last night and I haven't had a chance to tell you."

Then there is the modern story of the family who rented a beach house for the summer. As the children swam in the ocean and built castles in the sand, they noticed an old lady appear in the distance. Her gray hair was blowing in the wind and her clothes were ragged and she seemed to be muttering to herself as she bent over and picked up things from the beach and put them in a bag.

One youngster whispered, "Look! A witch." And the kids ran up to the beach house. The parents warned the children to stay away from the old lady. But every day, like clockwork, the old lady walked by the house on the beach, bending over, picking up things. She often smiled at the people who lived there but received only a stony glare in reply.

The day the family left the house, they were turning over the key to the owner when the old lady passed by again. "Who is she?" they asked. "Oh," the owner said, "she's just a little old lady whose life crusade is to pick up bits of glass from the beach so kids won't cut their feet."

Unwanted Crosses

Just when everything looks good—just when your life seems calm for a change—something or someone comes along and turns it into a soap opera. Why can't things be simple? Why do we seem to be always carrying an unwanted cross?

How many times in your life have you looked heavenward and asked, "Why me, God?" We wonder who these people are who suddenly edge their way into our lives and turn serenity into ugliness. And we wonder about sickness and pain and sorrow. Sometimes we wonder if God is punishing us.

Many times we actually punish ourselves by inviting problems. . .emotional, psychological, physical. Other times we find ourselves caught up in problems caused by other people, and somehow, things just go from bad to worse.

Have you ever watched a gardener with a green thumb prune a rosebush? When he's through it looks as though the plant has been demolished, but he's really gotten rid of the dead wood. Without the pruning, the bush would deteriorate and no longer would the roses bloom. But soon, everything will be coming back to life.

This is pretty much what we have to do in life. Have the courage to get rid of the dead wood—the people and problems that make us feel we're deteriorating. And we musn't ever feel that God is punishing us for something we did. What God is telling us is that if we accept what life deals out to us, we can come out of our trouble a better person than we would have been without it.

It's very, very hard to say to yourself, "This is terrible right now, but God moves in mysterious ways. Maybe it's all for the best." But say it anyway. It will strengthen your soul.

The "No Excuse" Sunday

Several people have sent me different versions of a ficticious announcement they found in various church bulletins called "No Excuse Sunday." I offer herewith my own edited version:

In order to make it possible for everyone to attend church next week, we are planning a special No Excuse Sunday.

1. Cots will be provided in the vestibule for those who say, "Sunday is my only day for sleeping in."
2. Eye drops will be available for those whose eyes are tired from watching "Saturday Night Live."
3. We will issue steel helmets for those who believe the roof will cave in if they show up for church.
4. Blankets will be furnished for those who complain the church is too cold and fans will be distributed to those who say the church is too warm.
5. There will be hearing aids for those who say the pastor doesn't talk loud enough and ear plugs for those who say he talks too loud.
6. Scorecards will be provided for those who wish to count the hypocrites in church.
7. TV dinners will be available to those who claim they can't go to church and cook dinner, too.
8. One section of the church will have some trees and grass for those who say they best see God in nature—especially on the golf course.

And as the pièce de résistance,

9. The sanctuary will be decorated with both Christmas poinsettias and Easter lilies to create a familiar environment for those who have never seen the church without them.

Therefore...no excuses.

Having a Chat with the Lord

Back in the 1940's, two great playwrights, George S. Kaufman and Moss Hart, collaborated on a comedy that was pretty revolutionary for its time. It was called *You Can't Take It With You*—the story of a hopelessly whacky family headed by old Grandpa Vanderhof whose very practical view of life drove members of the establishment crazy.

A big laugh always came whenever the family sat down to dinner and Grandpa said grace. He clasped his hands, looked up and started the prayer with "Well, sir. . ." and then recited the good things that happened that day. His prayer was a little radical for its time, but there was absolutely nothing wrong with the way Grandpa Vanderhof addressed his God. It was Grandpa's way.

Some people are quite self-conscious when it comes to praying in their own words. I suggest they use the Lord's Prayer. Most people have committed it to memory and can recite it by rote. And when you recite it—*think* about what you're saying. It's a prayer of praise, acknowledgment, forgiveness, and deliverance from evil. It positions the petitioner as one who wants to live for God.

In time, you'll expand your repertoire to include prayers of thanks, prayers of petition, and prayers of the heart. In time, your children will imitate you and begin to pray.

Speaking of that, a mother was a trifle worried about her little boy's salutation before bedtime. He would say, "Hi, God! I'm Christopher!" Don't worry, Mom, God appreciates Christopher's exhuberance.

Parables on Prayer

*T*here are, of course, many more religions than my own—religions that call for more stringent life-styles, religions that make ritualistic demands that Americans might find inconvenient, to say the least.

You have to admire the devout of other faiths who crawl on their knees up the steps of their temples, who fast for many days while observing their own holy days. And in the tenets that make up their religions are little gems of philosophy that I find fascinating.

The rule in one Indian monastery was *not* "Do not speak," but, "Do not speak unless you can improve on the silence." Gandhi put it this way: "It is better in prayer to have a heart without words than words without a heart."

One Indian parable tells of an old man who would sit motionless for hour after hour in his church. One day a priest asked him what he talked to God about. "I don't talk to God," the old man said. "I just listen." "Well then," the priest asked, "what does God say to you?" And the man said, "God doesn't talk, either." He just listens."

Another of these Indian parables on prayer says, "There are four stages of prayer. First: I talk, you listen. Second: You talk, I listen. Third: Neither talks, both listen. Fourth: Neither talks, neither listens. Silence."

I believe what these profound teachings imply is that we need to learn how to "waste time" with

God, nature, ourselves, our family, our jobs. This quietness before God and God's creation can only deepen us and lead to balance and peace. We will find the mystery of our lives once again.

For God speaks to the human heart without words.

Facing Tomorrow

*I*t happens to a lot of us. We start worrying about something we'll have to face and deal with in the next few days. It's unnerving. You wish it would go away.

The best thing you can do is concentrate on today, because you must live this day, too. This advice is as old as the hills, but it still applies. Say to yourself, "Just for today, I will try to live through this day and not try to tackle my whole life at once." And *believe* you can!

The difference between a believer and a non-believer is that the believer, in the midst of crisis, looks for meaning and finds ways to survive the suffering. The non-believer despairs. The key is to trust yourself and trust in your God.

In his *Introduction to the Devout Life*, St. Francis de Sales put it very well. It's almost poetry:

> Do not fear what may happen to you tomorrow. The same Father who cares for you today will care for you tomorrow and every other day. Either he will shield you from suffering or he will give you unfailing strength to bear it. Be at peace, then, and put aside all anxious thoughts and imaginings.

There is no mysticism in what I have written and reported in this book. These are the things you talk about over a cup of coffee. These are the little events that, whether it's obvious or not, envelop the presence of God.

I have shared them to help you feel a little better about yourself, your family, your friends, your job, nature, and, of course, your life. Above all, it is my *hope* that they have given you...great hope.

Just remember that line: "Put aside all anxious thoughts and imaginings."

Your friend,

Thomas Hartman

About the Author

Monsignor Thomas Hartman is a man clearly born to serve. Ordained a Catholic priest in 1971, he received his B.A. in Philosophy and M.A. in Theology from Niagara University, a M.Div. from Our Lady of Angels Seminary in Albany, and a Doctorate of Ministry from the Jesuit School of Theology, Berkeley, CA—and is the recipient of several honorary degrees as well.

Enthusiastic, outgoing, dynamic, community involved, and future oriented, "Father Tom," as he is popularly known, is now one of the most widely respected religious figures in the media. He is especially well known for his radio broadcast, "Journies through Rock," as well as his cable television programs, "The God Squad," "TeLIcare Tonight," and "Faithline."

Additionally, he maintains an extensive lecture schedule and speaks before varied audiences on the subject of media as well as topics of interest to the medical community, family groups/organizations, parishes, students, and counselors. Hartman also has strong active ties with the business community and holds many professional board memberships, including Long Island Housing Partnership, Long Island Council on Alcoholism, and PBS-Channel 21.

Among his numerous awards are two Emmys, a Gabriel, and the Brotherhood Award bestowed by the National Conference of Christians and Jews.

In addition to several magazine articles, Hartman is co-author of the award-winning and popular book for parents and children, entitled *Where Does God Live?* Since 1979 he has been Director of Radio and TV for the Diocese of Rockville Centre, Long Island, NY.